strengths

Information Architecture

leadership

five levels

ntrol points

Corp ...sis

ional

culture of improvement

Lean Radar Chart

Corporate Diagnosis

partnerin

oard

CUSTOMER FOCUS

Delta Zero

business renewal process

Standardization

mass production

get/Means Diagram

Implementation Planning Sheet

Information Architecture

Lean Management System

cus team

Focus (Phase I)

Monthly Planner

adherence (Phase III)

lean equipment management

Delta Zero

R D

action team

provemnt Cycle

Reflection (Phase IV)

lean organization

checkpoints

ts

system excellence

structure

ganizational learning

X-Type Matrix

Corporate Diagnosis

Corporate Diagnosis

SETTING THE GLOBAL STANDARD FOR EXCELLENCE

THOMAS L. JACKSON

with Constance E. Dyer

Publisher's Message by Norman Bodek

PRODUCTIVITY PRESS

Portland, Oregon

Productivity Press
P.O. Box 13390
Portland OR 97213-0390
United States of America
Telephone: 503-235-0600
Telefax: 503-235-0909
E-mail: service@ppress.com

Cover design by William Stanton
Cover photograph by Bob Waldman
Page design by Shannon Holt
Page composition and graphics by Rohani Design, Edmonds, Washington
Printed and bound by Edwards Brothers in the United States of America

Library of Congress Cataloging-in-Publication Data

Jackson, Thomas Lindsay, 1949–
    Corporate diagnosis : setting the global standard for excellence / Thomas L. Jackson with Constance E. Dyer
        p. cm.
    Includes bibliographical references and index.
    ISBN 1-56327-086-2 (hardcover)
    1. Total quality management. 2. Industrial productivity—Evaluation. 2. Performance technology. 3. Strategic planning. I. Dyer, Constance E., 1947– II. Title.
    HD62.15.J34 1995
    658.5'62--dc20   95-34927
                                                               CIP

01 00 99 98 97 96   10 9 8 7 6 5 4 3 2 1

to Hemant, Kalyani, Sunaina, and Miheka

Nothing endures but change.
—Heraclitus

Contents

PUBLISHER'S MESSAGE ix
ACKNOWLEDGMENTS xv

1. INTRODUCTION 1

Where Corporate Diagnosis Fits in the Lean Management System 2
Who Conducts the Corporate Diagnosis? 5
Diagnostic Questions 6
Lean Management Progress Tables 6
Concordances with Major Prize Criteria and Implementation Systems 7
Corporate Diagnosis Charts and Forms 7
The Diagnostic Scoring System 8

2. A LEAN MANAGEMENT SYSTEM OVERVIEW 9

Development Framework 10
    Three Cornerstones of Growth 10
    Nine Keys to Development 12
        Control Points 15
    Five Levels of Organizational Learning 15
The Business Renewal Process 18
The Strategic Improvement Cycle 20
Delta Zero 23

3. **STEPS IN CORPORATE DIAGNOSIS** 27

Preparation 28
    Development of Questions 29
        Question Preparation Aids 29
        Which Keys to Consider 31
        Scheduling the Diagnosis 33
    Report from the Unit Diagnosed 33
The Diagnostic Site Visit 34
    Preparing the Diagnostic Form 34
    Recording Observations 37
Analysis, Scoring, and Short-Term Prescription 39
Recognition of Achievement 39
Key Points in Work Unit Diagnosis 40

4. **DIAGNOSTIC SCORING** 41

Using the Progress Tables for Scoring 41
Using the Scoring Criteria 42
    Reliable Method 44
    Extent of Deployment 45
    Extent of Cross-Functional Integration 46
    Results 46
The Diagnostic Scoring Matrix 46
Reaching a Companywide Score 46
    The Lean Management Scoreboard 48
    The Lean Radar Chart 51

APPENDIX A: Diagnostic Questions and Lean Management Progress
           Tables 53

APPENDIX B: Concordances to Major Productivity and Quality Awards 95

FOR FURTHER READING 109
ABOUT THE AUTHORS 111
INDEX 113

Publisher's Message

MANY COMPANY LEADERS ARE DISCOVERING that the world is getting smaller these days. Low-cost overseas competitors are coming up with quality innovations in their markets and closing the delivery gap. The effective response to this is *learning,* in every dimension:

- learning what the customers really value
- learning how world class rivals and noncompetitors are producing and delivering that value
- learning your company's position and what human and machine technology *needs to be learned companywide* to produce and deliver customer value better than anyone else
- learning to measure the company's success and stay on the winning course, year after year

Over the years, Productivity has taught many effective tools and methods for delivering customer value. In *Corporate Diagnosis,* we present a method for systematically measuring the success of such initiatives as part of a companywide improvement process.

This book is about knowing the score in your company. Corporate Diagnosis is a powerful way to understand your company's capabilities and track its progress against benchmarks set by world leaders in lean management. Going beyond the previous business results on which most companies base their policy decisions, Corporate Diagnosis gives you a systemic perspective of the company's status with its customers and competitors. Corporate Diagnosis rounds out the financials with an assessment of how well the company is achieving its current objectives and its goals for future growth and competitiveness.

Learning the score is followed by top management activities to determine what's most important to improve next, and then by companywide activities to make the change. Every year another diagnosis is conducted to see how well the company learned and developed, continuing the plan-do-check-act cycle of improvement. Corporate Diagnosis and the planning and improvement cycle are critical activities in the Lean Management System (described in detail in a companion volume, *Implementing a Lean Management System*).

Lean management is about operating the most efficient and effective organization possible, with the least cost and zero waste. It is an approach that requires companies to make smart use of their resources—their technology, their equipment, and especially the knowledge and skills of their people. Above all, lean management is about running an intelligent business, in which everyone from the shop floor to top management is aware of the company's capabilities and ensures that they are used appropriately and continually improved.

In helping companies master the lean management process, we have identified nine key areas of organizational learning that companies must measure and develop to secure their futures:

- Customer focus
- Leadership
- Lean organization
- Partnering
- Information architecture
- Culture of improvement
- Lean production
- Lean equipment management
- Lean engineering

Each of these interrelated keys breaks down into a set of more specific control points and checkpoints that help determine how to measure progress.

During the annual improvement cycle, top management determines which key areas to focus on and sets broad targets, then deploys the targets to the rest of the organization to make more concrete. Toward the end of the improvement cycle, top management uses Corporate Diagnosis to review how various parts of the company have challenged their targets and to score the development of the entire company in the nine key areas.

Numerical results are only part of the scoring in Corporate Diagnosis. To accurately determine the company's "lean quotient," managers also reflect on three other criteria:

- the company's systematic use of world class methods
- the deployment of methods throughout the company
- the cross-functional integration of the company in its methods and management

Companies are scored on a five-level spectrum of development ranging from traditional mass production to lean management excellence. These levels are like five stages of making a garden. First the ground is prepared, then certain areas are planted; with weeding and new planting a complete landscape develops, and ultimately it becomes a flourishing interconnected organism. Like a mature garden, an integrated lean organization is not built overnight, but through dedicated analysis, planning, and effort over time.

To keep the game interesting to all the players, scores are shared throughout the company on radar charts. These visual displays give everyone an instant picture of the current level of achievement and the company's ultimate goals, encouraging the effort to reduce waste and hit the lean management bull's-eye.

Chapter 1 of the book describes Corporate Diagnosis in the context of the Lean Management System and tells who needs to be involved for optimum results. It introduces the main elements of diagnosis, including the Diagnostic Questions, the Progress Tables, and the scoring system.

Chapter 2 is an overview of the Lean Management System, geared for managers who have not yet read *Implementing a Lean Management System.*

Chapter 3 takes the reader step-by-step through the audit process, from the preliminary questions to the site visit, scoring discussion, and celebration of progress. It gives guidelines for using the Progress Tables and Diagnostic Questions to develop company-specific substantive questions for the diagnosis.

Chapter 4 tells how to use the Progress Tables to interpret the observations and identify unit scores for each lean management control point. In addition, four generalized scoring criteria are presented in matrix form to help fine-tune the unit scores and determine companywide results. Various score-recording aids are introduced, including lean management radar charts.

Appendix A contains the Diagnostic Questions and Progress Tables for each of the Lean Management System control points. It should be emphasized that these questions and tables are truly the heart of the Lean Management System. Although we have grouped them in an appendix for ease of use, these materials are not peripheral to the process described in the chapters. The information they present is a rich and well-rounded essence that has been refined from our experience with companies at various levels of lean management development and with many different approaches to measuring that development. The symptoms shown in the Progress Tables are actually learning objectives that build from level to level, offering step-by-step directions for reaching lean management excellence. The questions and tables give a physical and conceptual picture of what a company will experience as it develops lean and profitable management. Study them carefully.

Appendix B is a useful Table of Concordances that links the Lean Management System control points with similar sections of the criteria of the world's major productivity and quality awards used by many companies to structure their improvement strategies. Included are the Baldrige Award, the Shingo Prize, the Deming Application Prize, and the PM Prize. Sections of Hiroyuki Hirano's *JIT Implementation Manual* and Iwao Kobayashi's *20 Keys to Workplace Improvement* are also linked to the Lean Management System.

This book will give you the framework for conducting a Corporate Diagnosis in your own organization. However, although it offers numerous guidelines, forms, and sample questions, it is not a recipe to simply "plug in" to your situation. To get meaningful feedback from this review, you must tailor it to fit your company and your market. Customers in different markets value different things in their suppliers; you need to frame your questions and scoring in terms of what your customers want now and may want in the future—and what kind of organization must be in place to provide those outputs. Likewise, the Progress Tables we share as scoring aids offer some concrete measures based on the experiences of lean, world class companies—but the definition of world class is continually refined and improved. It is important to stay up to date on the results and methods of the best in class in your own business. Ultimately, you want your company to be the one setting that standard.

Productivity, Inc. has been teaching the elements of lean management and lean production since the late 1970s when the company first led study missions to Toyota and other Japanese industrial leaders, and brought to the West the ideas of Shigeo Shingo, developer of the Toyota production system. Since that time our consultants, trainers, and publications have helped thousands of companies in the United States and around the world learn how to implement lean methods, and we have learned in turn from their experiences. This book represents the distillation of many years of experience with the world's best strategies for manufacturing, and we are pleased to share it with you.

We express our appreciation to Tom Jackson for bringing his wisdom and experience to develop this diagnostic approach and to Connie Dyer for her substantial contribution to the definition of lean management key areas and control points, and to the Progress Tables. Thanks also to Diane Asay, editor in chief for Productivity Press, who valued this project and encouraged its development. Development editor Karen Jones gave helpful input and feedback in organizing and clarifying the text and illustrations. Vivina Ree provided essential editorial work on the rough manuscript. Productivity Press art director Bill Stanton created the cover design and Gretchen Long designed the endpapers. The pages were designed by Shannon Holt, and art and type were composed by Rohani Design. Susan Swanson managed the prepress, with editorial assistance from Pauline Sullivan. Catchword, Inc. created the index.

Norman Bodek
Publisher

Acknowledgments

CORPORATE DIAGNOSIS IS BASED ON a level-by-level approach to the development and improvement of business systems that is widely applied in Japan and is followed by leading companies in the United States. The elements of this approach have been adapted from numerous sources, including Iwao Kobayashi's *20 Keys to Workplace Improvement,* Hiroyuki Hirano's *JIT Implementation Manual,* Yoji Akao's *Hoshin Kanri,* and Alberto Galgano's *Companywide Quality Management.* In addition, we have drawn from the criteria of the world's major quality and productivity awards, including the Deming Application Prize, the PM Prize (TPM implementation), and the TP Management Prize, as well as the Malcolm Baldrige National Quality Award and the Shingo Prize for Excellence in Manufacturing.

Tom Jackson

CHAPTER 1

Introduction

IN THE YEARS SINCE THE END of World War II a gradual revolution in manufacturing has been changing how the world makes and delivers goods and services. It is called lean production. Companies that have tried to implement lean production recognize that there is more to it than just applying the well-known methodologies imported from Japan. Approaches like just-in-time inventory control, quick changeover, mistake-proofing, total productive maintenance, and total quality management are powerful, but many companies fail to achieve the synergy they hope for in applying them. This is most often due to a lack of a logical and integrated implementation sequence that starts from where the company actually is and moves systematically toward the company's long-term business goals.

The Lean Management System fills this gap by providing a link between traditional strategic planning and the requirements for sustainable lean production. Just as important it connects the long-term development plan with daily improvement activities throughout the company.

A key step in the Lean Management System is a comprehensive diagnostic system called Corporate Diagnosis—a practical approach to company assessment that helps CEOs and management teams focus on what their companies must do to become more competitive. Corporate

Diagnosis continually benchmarks the company's strategic management system, its organizational structure, and its core strengths against the best practices and the best companies in the world. Whatever industry a company is in, whatever its approach to being the best in the marketplace, Corporate Diagnosis will help the company grow.

The Corporate Diagnosis should not be confused with technical audits such as product quality audits or ISO 9000 quality system audits. Corporate Diagnosis was first used in the early 1950s at Shin-Etsu Chemical Industry, a Japanese company that won the Deming Prize in 1953. Toyota Motor Company adopted the practice in 1962 as part of its implementation of companywide quality management. World class companies have institutionalized the Corporate Diagnosis and perform it at least once a year. Early in the process of introduction, companies often perform the diagnosis twice a year.

WHERE CORPORATE DIAGNOSIS FITS IN THE LEAN MANAGEMENT SYSTEM

This book is a companion volume to *Implementing a Lean Management System,* which maps out a comprehensive management system that supports lean production by aligning the firm's vision, strategy, structure, and capabilities with market realities. Readers unfamiliar with that book should study Chapter 2 of this work for an overview of the features of the Lean Management System. For those reading the two books together the following paragraphs will suffice to review the general framework.

The Lean Management System begins with a process of business renewal, in which the company assesses its competitiveness and plans for the future. The top management team augments its traditional strategic plan with a customer-focused vision and a long-term plan to develop the firm's technical and human resources. During the Business Renewal Process, a Corporate Diagnosis is done to set a baseline for the Development Plan.

Next, the top management team makes the company's vision and strategy concrete by initiating a Strategic Improvement Cycle with four phases, as shown in Figure 1-1.

In Phase I, Focus, the management team translates its business renewal strategy into a short-term (usually annual) policy, assigning concrete targets and responsibilities that can be easily understood by middle managers and

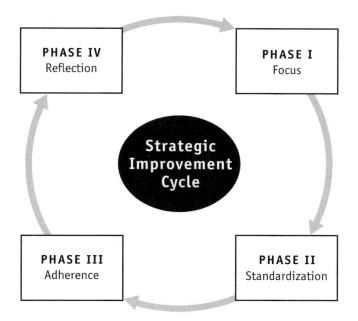

FIGURE 1-1.
THE STRATEGIC IMPROVEMENT CYCLE

employees. In Phase II, Standardization, the company deploys the policy targets and means to all managers and frontline team leaders, who in turn work with their employees to implement the policy by building increasingly specific targets and performance measures into daily work. During Phase III, Adherence, the company monitors improvement through managerial reports of work unit activities and results. Toward the end of the annual cycle, another Corporate Diagnosis is done to verify policy implementation and identify the current level of development. Finally, in Phase IV, Reflection, company leaders prepare for the next year's improvement cycle by analyzing discrepancies between targets and actual performance, reviewing the development indicated by the Corporate Diagnosis, and identifying changes in the firm or business environment that challenge assumptions made in the previous Business Renewal Process.

The focal point of a Corporate Diagnosis is the CEO's diagnosis, a formal top management audit during which the company leaders verify personally that the firm's strategy and operational policies have been deployed and implemented successfully. The purpose of top-level audits is to diagnose the strategic condition of the company. Hence, the top management audit has come to be called a "diagnosis" because management is checking the company's "pulse"—its progress toward the fit and healthy state of lean management. Company leaders use the Corporate Diagnosis process to look for signs of organizational health or dysfunction and follow their assessment by prescribing corrective actions.

The goals of the Corporate Diagnosis are threefold:

- to check the consistency of each organizational unit's improvement projects and daily activities with company policy and long-term strategy
- to identify important gaps within the company and in the competitive environment
- to promote the development of world class capabilities

Corporate Diagnosis turns strategic planning and implementation into a Plan-Do-Check-Act cycle that assures the company of the right strategy, structure, and strengths for long-term organizational health. Using Corporate Diagnosis should help the leadership of any company keep score on how well the company is building its capabilities and competitive advantages for the future.

In practice, the top management Corporate Diagnosis is conducted near the end of the annual Strategic Improvement Cycle and is preceded by two levels of ongoing analysis and reporting:

- Action team reports
- Deployment team reports

Action team reports. In the Lean Management System, actual improvement work is directed by action teams composed of shopfloor managers, team leaders, and staff. Each action team is led or co-led by one or more midlevel area managers. Action teams manage the work toward specific targets handed to them by higher-level management teams called deployment teams, made up of action team leaders from various functions. As activities progress, action team leaders conduct daily and monthly reviews of the assigned improvement activities of workteams in their specific areas. At least monthly, the action team leaders submit status reports to apprise their deployment teams of progress and obstacles in implementation.

Deployment team reports. The deployment teams are led by members of the company's top management team (usually the head of a functional department). In the diagnostic process, their function is to respond to the action teams' information, and also to synthesize it, via monthly reports and annual audits, for the top management team that sets the company's annual policy and general targets. Deployment team leaders compile their target results and report them at top management meetings. These management reports set the stage for Corporate Diagnosis. The process in which they are used is described more fully in *Implementing a Lean Management System*.

WHO CONDUCTS THE CORPORATE DIAGNOSIS?

This book describes the audit process used by top management to assess every aspect of the company. Although we call this a "CEO's diagnosis" or "president's audit," in reality few individual CEOs or presidents have a sufficient grasp of the entire company to conduct this review without the assistance and wisdom of the functional and cross-functional leaders on the top management team. Chapter 3 offers guidelines for conducting team-based audits aimed at structured but open exchanges of opinions and ideas. This format should lead to better informed, more objective assessments of the company's achievements and challenges.

In small and even mid-sized companies, the chief executive and top management team may conduct the diagnosis for every area of the entire company. In larger companies, however, this process must be managed in stages. In such cases, teams of managers in charge of specific areas or functions perform preliminary audits of various work units. Since the Corporate Diagnosis is scored on the keys and control points of lean management, it makes sense for this managerial diagnosis to be conducted by the cross-functional deployment teams that defined and assigned the keys and control points during the Standardization phase of the Strategic Improvement Cycle. The reports and scores generated by these diagnostic teams are reviewed by top management before the formal CEO's diagnosis of the entire company. Even in smaller companies, the managers of various internal organizational units may find it useful to apply the Corporate

Diagnosis approach within units to better grasp their status. Chapter 3 gives guidelines for choosing appropriate questions for specific manufacturing functions.

Determining the scores for the entire company is not simply a matter of averaging work unit scores and coming up with a few magic numbers. The CEO and top management team need to conduct their own assessment of the health of the entire company in the areas that are important to future development. The CEO's diagnosis should not be a mere formality, but a substantive analysis that takes company leaders into the workplace to see for themselves how things are. Their question lists and site visits may be shorter if they follow unit-level assessments, but they should conduct their own inquiry to determine a company score in each key and control point. It is critical for the CEO and other company leaders to be personally aware of the state of their own company.

DIAGNOSTIC QUESTIONS

A major feature of the book is a set of generic diagnostic questions, which appear in the form of reference charts in Appendix A. Drawn from our experience working with organizations striving to achieve lean management, these questions touch on the systems and methods companies require to excel. As such, the questions serve as a prescriptive framework for a lean management system. These generic questions will be most useful when used as models or starting points from which to tailor questions that address the company's specific circumstances. In answering these questions frankly and systematically, management teams will develop a well-balanced perspective on the key factors, processes, and systems the company needs to work on to be a strong, lean competitor.

LEAN MANAGEMENT PROGRESS TABLES

As an aid to diagnosis, we have also prepared Progress Tables, which appear below the related questions in the charts in Appendix A. These tables help you gauge your company's status by evaluating specific characteristics or symptoms you can observe. The Progress Table criteria are the embodiment of the Lean Management System, distilled from our experience with companies at various levels of lean management development, and with different approaches to measuring that development. The symptoms shown in the Progress Tables are actually learning objectives that build from level to level, offering step-by-step directions for reaching lean management excellence.

Like the Diagnostic Questions, the Progress Tables are generic, but they suggest concrete highlights to look for in each key in a developing company. Most companies need several years of experience in lean management implementation before they accumulate enough information to make their own company-specific charts; during the startup period, the Progress Tables offer a useful framework for shaping diagnostic questions and for analyzing the answers. Although these questions and tables were originally developed in a manufacturing context, most of the control points have applications in the service sector as well.

CONCORDANCES WITH MAJOR PRIZE CRITERIA AND IMPLEMENTATION SYSTEMS

Many companies begin the process of integrating their world class initiatives by applying or adapting an existing framework. Frequently used models include the criteria of leading prizes for quality or productivity, such as the Malcolm Baldrige National Quality Award, or of lean production implementation systems such as those in Hiroyuki Hirano's *JIT Implementation Manual* or Iwao Kobayashi's *20 Keys to Workplace Improvement*. To help managers synchronize lean management with their application of these important frameworks, we have brought the relevant cross-references together in Concordances in Appendix B.

CORPORATE DIAGNOSIS CHARTS AND FORMS

To make the diagnosis easy to apply, we introduce forms for use during the audit and the scoring discussions. These include a blank Diagnostic Form for recording audit notes, a Lean Management Scoreboard for tallying control point scores within each key, and a Lean Radar Chart for visually displaying the company's level of development in all of the keys. These forms are used to record and chart the company's development through multiple rounds of the Strategic Improvement Cycle.

THE DIAGNOSTIC SCORING SYSTEM

The scoring system for measuring a company's development is described in Chapter 4. Implementing lean management is not a "yes-no" proposition in which a bureaucratic company suddenly becomes "lean." The system takes time to implement and various pieces will be developed at different times. Recognizing this, Corporate Diagnosis employs the Progress Tables and a Diagnostic Scoring Matrix to help managers position the company or work unit along a five-level scale of organizational learning and development, ranging from traditional mass production to a fully integrated lean management system. (These levels of learning are further described in Chapter 2.)

Some companies apply diagnostic scoring in the context of a company-wide certification program, particularly in relation to lean production and lean equipment management. Production or management units are scored at a certain level during periodic reviews and then strive to achieve certification to the next higher level by demonstrating achievement of certain agreed-on objective criteria.

CHAPTER 2

A Lean Management System Overview

IMPLEMENTING LEAN MANAGEMENT MEANS breaking old patterns and installing new ones. To accomplish this, an organization needs a whole new set of tools and a framework for applying them. It needs a *system*.

The dictionary defines a system as "a regularly interacting or interdependent group of items forming a unified whole"; "an organized set of doctrines, ideas, or principles"; "an organized or established procedure"; or "a manner of classifying, symbolizing, or schematizing."[1]

The Lean Management System captures all of these elements. It merges

- a strong but flexible conceptual architecture
- with specific application tools
- to form an integrated whole
- that aligns the various parts of an organization
- to make a change of great magnitude.

This chapter presents an overview of the building blocks and tools of the Lean Management System.

The backbone of the Lean Management System is a carefully constructed conceptual architecture that supports the structural, interpersonal, external, and internal relationships governing a company's operations. It has three main elements: the development framework, the Business Renewal Process, and Strategic Improvement Cycles.

DEVELOPMENT FRAMEWORK

The development framework comprises several key components:

- Three cornerstones of growth
- Nine keys to development
- Five levels of organizational learning

These structural elements have been developed to refine management's thinking about how to define, build, and manage their organizations.

The development framework is supported by a Business Renewal Process that creates a long-term Development Plan for the organization, and by multiple rounds of the lean management Strategic Improvement Cycle, which turns the Development Plan into action.

The force that animates all of these elements and propels them toward an ideal, waste-free state is Delta Zero.

Three Cornerstones of Growth

The Lean Management System is structured around three necessities of lean production: strategic planning, organizational structure, and human resource capabilities. These three necessities are distilled into a working concept which the Lean Management System calls the *three cornerstones of growth,* or *Strategy, Structure,* and *Strengths* (see Figure 2-1). While all companies have these three elements, just as all buildings have a foundation, walls, and infrastructure, a lean company is aware of their existence and features, and will organize its growth around them. A carpenter who knows a building's foundation, material, and structure has much greater success in remodeling than one who doesn't. A lean company that wants to grow must first have a clear sense of its own strategy, structure, and strengths.

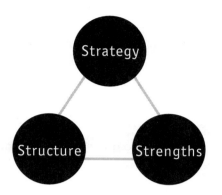

FIGURE 2-1.
THE THREE CORNERSTONES OF GROWTH

Strategy refers to strategic intent—the kind of business the company aims to be—and to a plan of action. The right strategy will match the business's unique strengths with the most valuable customer segments in the right markets, spelling out the development of its structure and strengths over time. The point of all strategic planning is to prepare the business for the future. In a Lean Management System, *customer focus* and *leadership* are key features of a company's strategy.

Structure refers to how the business's internal and external relations are arranged, as well as to the flow of information within the total organization, both internal and external. An appropriate structure ensures that the individuals and institutions involved in product development, production, and distribution will communicate and cooperate efficiently and flexibly. In a lean company, *lean organization, partnering,* and *information architecture* hold up this second growth cornerstone.

Strengths refers to organizational capabilities or step-by-step production and support routines mastered by the company, through which it gets work done. The appropriate mix of strengths ensures that strategy can be executed and a broad range of structural possibilities expressed. The right strengths ensure a readiness and responsiveness to changes in the competitive environment, whether anticipated or sudden. A company's *improvement culture, production system, equipment management,* and *engineering* control its capabilities, or strengths.

Nine Keys to Development

Managing strategy, structure, and strengths is easier said than done, especially under conditions of rapid change. In mass production organizations, these three attributes are products of past development processes based on old assumptions about the future. Without a correct and clear view of the future, change can disconnect a firm's strategy, structure, and strengths, spinning a company into organizational turmoil. More often than not, old-style business leaders concentrate narrowly on financial aspects of strategy, failing to consider the company's structure or strengths. What frequently results is a disconnected strategy with an outmoded structure and inadequate operational strengths.

To ensure a more holistic approach to development of policy, the Lean Management System has developed a flexible and controlled response to change through what we call the nine keys to development. Each key (italicized in the previous section) regulates one of the growth cornerstones—strategy, structure, or strengths (see Figure 2-2). Each key is associated with a particular zero-waste goal. Figure 2-3 summarizes how the keys and their zero-waste goals improve profitability.

The nine keys form the main categories in which an organization charts its progress. A drive to build or improve the nine keys distinguishes a lean from a mass producer. Implementers should note that these keys are not set in stone; we expect that our own system will continue to evolve and that implementers will develop new keys to meet their own particular needs.

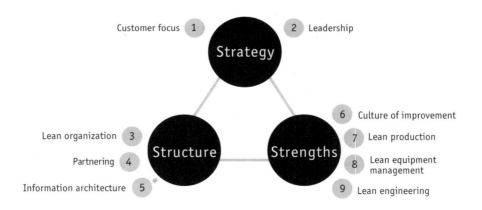

FIGURE 2-2.
THE NINE KEYS TO DEVELOPMENT

Key	Zero-Waste Goal	Relation to Profit
1. Customer focus	Zero customer dissatisfaction	Customer input and feedback assures quality. Customer satisfaction supports sales.
2. Leadership	Zero misalignment	Direction and support for development improves cost, quality, and speed.
3. Lean organization	Zero bureaucracy	Team-based operations reduce overhead by eliminating bureaucracy and ensuring information flow and cooperation.
4. Partnering	Zero stakeholder dissatisfaction	Flexible relationships with suppliers, distributors, and society improve quality, cost, and speed.
5. Information architecture	Zero lost information	Knowledge required for operations is accurate and timely, thus improving quality, cost, and speed.
6. Culture of improvement	Zero wasted creativity	Employee participation in eliminating operations waste improves cost, quality, and speed.
7. Lean production	Zero non-value-adding work	Total employee involvement and aggressive waste elimination promote speedier operations and eradicate inventories.
8. Lean equipment management	Zero failures, zero defects	Longer equipment life and design improvement reduce cost. Meticulous maintenance and equipment improvement increase quality. Absolute availability and efficiency increase speed.
9. Lean engineering	Zero lost opportunity	Early resolution of design problems with customers and suppliers significantly reduces cost, while improving quality and cycle time.

FIGURE 2-3.
HOW THE NINE KEYS IMPROVE PROFITABILITY

The Strategic Keys. The two keys to building an effective strategy are customer focus and leadership. Mastery of these keys will keep a company from being blindsided by unexpected customer demands and failing to develop capabilities to satisfy new demands.

Key 1. *Customer Focus* refers to the feedback processing methods that inform a company what the customer wants and ensure that it is delivered. When the customer dreams of something, the company will know it and—if all other keys are in top gear—the customer will get it. Since customer satisfaction is the straightest road to profit, its impact on profitability is direct. The impact of this key penetrates an entire business, from design to production to delivery. *Goal: zero customer dissatisfaction.*

Key 2. *Leadership* is the management team's ability to translate customer requirements into concrete policies, organizational structures, and production strengths. This key's relationship to profit is critical, as illustrated by the way leadership, in providing direction and support for overall company development, improves cost, quality, and speed. *Goal: zero misalignment between strategy and human resources.*

The Structural Keys. Mastering these structural keys will ensure a flat, team-based organization that is well-integrated with suppliers and the environment, and in which vital information is always available at the point of use.

Key 3. *Lean Organization* is the structure of interlocking teams required to eliminate bureaucracy, minimize overhead, and promote responsiveness to market conditions. *Goal: zero bureaucracy.*

Key 4. *Partnering* is a set of conditions that must be effectively deployed to all stakeholders—employees, suppliers, and society at large to remain competitive. *Goal: zero stakeholder dissatisfaction.*

Key 5. *Information Architecture* structures the creation and distribution of information into a framework supportive of team-based organization. Architectural features include improvement-oriented performance measures and management accounting systems as well as the use of visual management. *Goal: zero lost information.*

The Keys to Strength. The keys to strength will ensure a workforce capable of improving any process and create a flexible production system; so that when the customer dreams of something new, the organization can deliver it in minimal time.

Key 6. *Culture of Improvement* equips teams and individual employees to analyze strategic gaps and quality problems to find their root causes, and then conceive, implement, and standardize effective solutions. *Goal: zero wasted creativity.*

Key 7. *Lean Production* includes the array of waste-reduction techniques such as quick changeover, JIT production methods, mistake-proofing, and other methods that help companies produce exactly what the customer wants, when it is wanted. *Goal: zero non-value-adding work.*

Key 8. *Lean Equipment Management* refers to a total productive maintenance (TPM) approach that ensures the efficiency, accuracy, and ease of operation and maintenance, as well as readiness and availability of equipment and systems. *Goal: zero failures, zero defects.*

Key 9. *Lean Engineering* refers to the practice of concurrent engineering and all necessary means to rapidly and consistently design and produce new products that delight customers. *Goal: zero lost opportunity.*

CONTROL POINTS

Each of the nine keys is composed of a set of control points, more specific topics in which the company's achievement will be measured. The control points are listed on the Lean Management Scoreboard, one of the outputs of the Corporate Diagnosis (see Figure 2-4, discussed further in Chapter 4). During deployment of the annual improvement policy, the control points in turn are broken down into even more specific checkpoints and targets for action.

Five Levels of Organizational Learning

What can't be measured can't be controlled. Tracking the progress in the nine keys requires a system of measurement. The Lean Management System establishes five levels of development for each key to help managers evaluate the organization's progress toward world class competitiveness:

Level Five	Mass production
Level Four	System initiation

CORPORATE DIAGNOSIS

CORNER-STONES OF GROWTH	KEYS TO DEVELOPMENT	CONTROL POINTS	5 Levels of Organizational Learning				
			Level 5	Level 4	Level 3	Level 2	Level 1
Strategy	1 Customer focus	1.1 Customer requirements					
		1.2 Customer relationships					
		1.3 Order-to-delivery process					
	2 Leadership	2.1 Business renewal					
		2.2 Focus					
		2.3 Standardization					
		2.4 Adherence					
		2.5 Reflection					
Structure	3 Lean organization	3.1 Team activities					
		3.2 Networked organization					
		3.3 Rewards + recognition					
		3.4 Evaluation + compensation					
		3.5 Lean administration					
	4 Partnering	4.1 Employee value					
		4.2 Comakership					
		4.3 Environmental impact					
		4.4 Social integrity					
	5 Information architecture	5.1 Workplace org. & vis. control					
		5.2 Fast feedback systems					
		5.3 Performance measurement					
		5.4 Kaizen reporting					
Strengths	6 Culture of improvement	6.1 Standardization					
		6.2 Waste-free strategy					
		6.3 Technology diffusion					
		6.4 Education					
	7 Lean production	7.1 Flow production					
		7.2 Multiprocess handling					
		7.3 Leveled, mixed model prod.					
		7.4 Quick changeover					
		7.5 Automation with a human touch					
		7.6 Pull system/coupled production					
		7.7 Production scheduling					
	8 Lean equipment management	8.1 Equip./process improvement					
		8.2 Autonomous maintenance					
		8.3 Planned maintenance					
		8.4 Quality maintenance					
		8.5 Early equipment management					
		8.6 Safety					
		8.7 Equip. invest./maint. prev. design					
	9 Lean engineering	9.1 Design process					
		9.2 Design for QCD					

Right-side summary markers:

$\overline{3} = \square$

$\overline{5} = \square$

$\overline{5} = \square$

$\overline{4} = \square$

$\overline{4} = \square$

$\overline{4} = \square$

$\overline{7} = \square$

$\overline{7} = \square$

$\overline{2} = \square$

FIGURE 2-4.
BLANK LEAN MANAGEMENT SCOREBOARD

Level Three	System development
Level Two	System maturity
Level One	System excellence

By definition lean management can never be truly mastered. A true world class competitor will always strive to improve, refine, and surpass today's achievements. The zero-waste goal target in each key area is continuously moving beyond one's grasp.

In each of the nine key areas, learning begins with a self-assessment of current conditions. A company that diagnoses itself as a mass production organization will strive to initialize lean management through focused pilot projects in critical operational areas. Having accomplished this task, management may reassess the company as a level four organization. Ascending to the next level requires the company to take what it has learned from its pilot projects and deploy it to all major operational areas, the successful completion of which will project the organization to level three lean status. The firm may next face the challenge of extending the new practices into all areas of operations, including support. Ascending to level two requires more skill than all previous efforts combined.

Success is defined as having achieved at least level three (system development) in all nine keys. Development from level five to level three can be fairly rapid in all keys; development from level three to levels two and one is much slower. Company size and other factors may affect the rate of development. Firms already far along in implementing various keys will require less time.

Once Lean Management Systems are fully matured at level two, graduation to world class competitor level requires the greatest effort of all. A notoriously tough college professor was once asked by a nervous student what it would take to earn an "A" in his class. The professor, peering over his glasses, replied, "To earn an 'A' in my class you have to teach me something." To reach level one in any of the nine keys, a company must be in the forefront of best practice. It must demonstrate refinement and originality, and provide a benchmark for other companies to follow. The Lean Management System can help a firm reach this state, but everyone in the organization must be prepared for a lot of hard work.

Development through the five levels is not always a smooth climb. The nine keys are linked in a single system: just as improvement in one key enables better performance in all others, poor performance in one key will hinder better performance in all others. Companies just starting on the path to lean production and management often realize for the first time how uneven their previous development has been. Many companies find that they have overdeveloped their engineering capabilities and underdeveloped their cultural and production capabilities.

It is virtually impossible for a company to develop each key with equally high investments of attention and intensity. Emphasizing two or three keys each year as focal areas for the company's improvement energy is what grows a company from year to year. In the Lean Management System, these two or three keys are referred to as *critical keys*. They are not necessarily the keys that are most important to the company's long-term strategy, but rather the ones that most need improvement to support progress in the others. These critical keys will shift from year to year depending on the company's focus during each strategic planning cycle. Identifying different critical keys each year adjusts the balance among strategy, structure, and strengths, and controls the rate and direction of the company's evolution.

Development can be controlled, but it often proceeds more slowly than we wish. Installing lean management technology is not like plugging in a machine and flicking the "on" switch. It is based on people, teamwork, and total employee involvement, and it requires time to implement, mature, and refine.

THE BUSINESS RENEWAL PROCESS

Lean companies reexamine their reason for existence on a regular basis and infuse the entire organization with the answer they develop. To eliminate waste of all kinds, a lean company involves its entire workforce in continuously reengineering its production processes and ultimately redefines the industry by the way it does things. Such cultures of improvement encourage quantum leaps in improvement innovation. Toyota's development of just-in-time production was just such a leap. The attitude of improvement so permeates lean companies today that quantum leaps are a regular occurrence. Toyota's development of the Lexus, a new standard in the luxury car market, is a case in point. A Lexus costs 15 to 30 percent less to manufacture than a comparable Mercedes-Benz. Hewlett-Packard's phenomenal printer business is another example of a quantum leap that

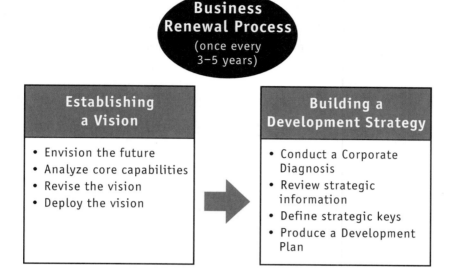

FIGURE 2-5.
THE BUSINESS RENEWAL PROCESS

redefined the industry. Through a combination of technical innovation and drastic cost reduction, HP now dominates the market for personal ink-jet and laser printers.

Lean producers not only reengineer their production processes, they redesign, reinvent, and reengineer entire businesses on a schedule. Using breakthrough thinking, lean companies compete on the basis of surprise, by creating a stream of new product and production standards for their competitors. The process through which lean companies create the future is called the *Business Renewal Process* (see Figure 2-5). It requires a company to periodically start with a blank slate, and ask: Why are we in business at all?

The process of business renewal is closely related to traditional strategic planning. Using market forecasts, traditional strategic planning tries to ensure greater profits or stock prices by defining a product's variety, quality, markets, distribution, and prices. The Business Renewal Process continues these mainstays of traditional strategic planning, but also incorporates some innovations.

- First, the lean management Business Renewal Process is repeated whenever it's required, but at least every three to five years. This conscious decision to renew the organization's focus ensures that a company keeps pace with the shifting business climate—that is, changes in technology, best practices, and market conditions.
- Second, the first step in the Business Renewal Process is to define a far-reaching vision that focuses sharply on customers' needs and desires. The starting point is vision, rather than profit, because profit is merely a by-product of customer satisfaction. Profit analysis, though important, plays a secondary role.
- Third, the Business Renewal Process requires corporate management to generate a lean management Development Plan based on the nine keys. This will help build new organizational structures and strengths to match new visions and strategies.

Chapters 3 and 4 of *Implementing a Lean Management System* describe in detail the steps of the Business Renewal Process.

THE STRATEGIC IMPROVEMENT CYCLE

The Business Renewal Process is followed by several rounds of learning and improvement called *Strategic Improvement Cycles*. These annual or semi-annual cycles form a "policy bridge" between the vision and the specifics of implementation. Each cycle attacks specific areas that need attention, enabling a company to progress from one level to the next. By undergoing this process, the firm gradually will realize or come closer to its vision.

The strategic improvement cycle has four distinct phases (see Figure 2-6):

Phase I.   Focus. In this phase, a top management team devises an annual policy that focuses on improving two or three of the key areas. This policy helps the company concentrate its energies on closing critical strategic gaps.

Phase II.   Standardization. This phase standardizes policy, first, by deploying it to all managers, supervisors, and team leaders, and second, by involving all employees in its implementation through focused team activities and documentation.

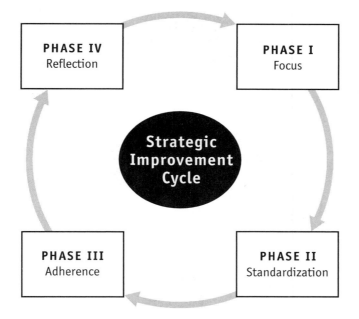

FIGURE 2-6.
THE STRATEGIC IMPROVEMENT CYCLE

> **Phase III. Adherence.** This phase assures a company's adherence
> to its business renewal strategy through a system of con-
> cise reports and an annual audit of policy implementa-
> tion, the *Corporate Diagnosis.*
> **Phase IV. Reflection.** In Phase IV, the top management team ana-
> lyzes performance for the previous period and reviews the
> company's capabilities, markets, and industry conditions.
> Based on this, it prioritizes problems and strategic chal-
> lenges to address, then revises policy in preparation for
> another cycle of strategic improvement.

These phases, described in Chapters 5 through 8 of *Implementing a Lean
Management System,* help a company assess its direction, learn from its mis-
takes, and build strong competitive strengths for success in the future. Each
phase involves processes that help teams prioritize and analyze problems,
and then develop, prioritize, and implement improvement ideas to achieve
the organization's strategic goals.

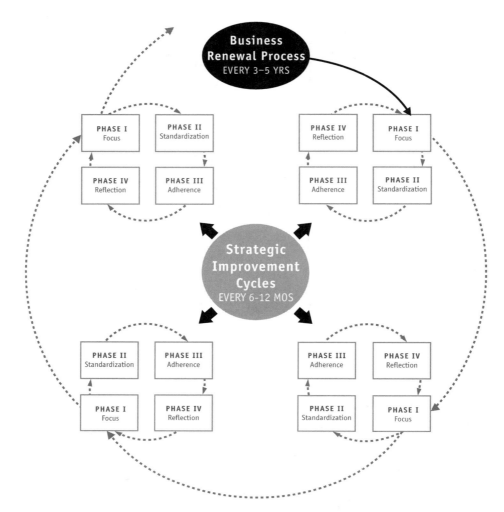

FIGURE 2-7.
A GRAPHIC MODEL OF THE BUSINESS RENEWAL PROCESS AND
STRATEGIC IMPROVEMENT CYCLES

The company repeats the Strategic Improvement Cycle until it reaches a certain level of improvement, then commences another Business Renewal Process. Figure 2-7 depicts how these cycles flow together in a spiral of improvement.

Normally, the Strategic Improvement Cycle is repeated once a year. Companies just beginning lean management may take up to 18 months to complete a cycle. Others operating in fast-moving markets may repeat the cycle twice within a year to accelerate organizational learning.

DELTA ZERO

Lean companies owe their success in part to maintaining zero waste in operations. Lean companies are unbeatable not merely because they are waste free, however, but because they expect the unexpected, and meet each new challenge with unexpected moves. Lean companies are innovative, flexible, agile. Being so far beyond their competitors' capabilities, the activities of lean companies are almost invisible to their contenders. When American manufacturers visited Japanese factories in the late 1970s, they literally could not see what was taking place before their eyes. Since these Western visitors did not know what to look for, innovations that could return billions of dollars in profit went unnoticed. The new techniques of management such as JIT and TPM sprang at them seemingly from nowhere. Likewise, competitors of lean organizations literally don't know where lean companies are coming from; it is as if these lean companies had disappeared into thin air, only to spring out when the time is right, with devastating effect. This ability to surprise is one small facet of the power of Delta Zero.

Delta Zero is the union of two concepts: *delta,* the Greek letter symbolizing incremental change, and *zero,* the Arabic numeral symbolizing void.

DELTA ZERO

Essentially, Delta Zero refers to the paradox of learning. All learning, personal as well as organizational, takes place on one of two levels:

- *Normal learning,* in which we add knowledge or increase performance incrementally within paradigms—fundamental structures of information that define the boundaries and structure of the various spheres in which we operate.
- *Paradigmatic learning,* in which we create new paradigms.

Without paradigms, our minds would be simply overwhelmed by the flood of information coming from our senses. Paradigms establish familiar mental norms we often take for granted. We usually do not question the paradigm in which our view of the universe is grounded; we merely extend or embellish that view. *Delta* is a good symbol for the structured learning that takes place within a normal, accepted paradigm.

A change in paradigm is always revolutionary, starting anew with a clean slate. Consider the development of new paradigms in science. Examples include Copernicus's idea that the planets revolve around the sun, Newton's discovery of the laws of motion and gravitation, and Einstein's theory of relativity. Like a baseline, *Zero* represents the creative force that stimulates new paradigms to emerge.

The two types of learning, normal and paradigmatic, are often in conflict. Old paradigms die hard. Because they affect so much of what we know and do, new paradigms are challenged simply in the interest of truth. Einstein's theory of relativity was not generally accepted until scientific observation confirmed several of the theory's predictions. Toyota's production system is only now spreading widely, after the sustained performance of Toyota and other lean companies has proved it beyond doubt. Moreover, people engaged in normal learning within an old paradigm often resist a new paradigm, even with clear evidence of validity, because change requires effort, or because they have vested interests in the old paradigm. Scientists sometimes resist new ideas because they can make old research (and reputations) obsolete. Within the business world, managers may resist new approaches because they imply change in organizational structure and loss of power.

For an organization to grow through learning, managers must grasp both the Delta—normal organizational learning—and the Zero—paradigmatic organizational learning. Managers must encourage learning within the existing paradigms of the customer and the process, while also preparing for business renewal and the adoption of new ideas. Because of the established nature of normal learning, new ideas frequently come from the fringes of the organization, or even from outside it.

The concept of Delta Zero is intended to ground management in both normal and paradigmatic learning simultaneously. Leaders must manage their paradigms to promote learning within the existing paradigm, to look out for valid new paradigms that will enhance organizational knowledge and competitiveness, and to manage the inevitable tension between the two approaches so that entrenched ideas do not stifle growth.

Delta Zero is both a principle and an attitude. As a principle, Delta Zero is a reminder that all things are in constant flux. Change is a given. A company that anticipates change from unexpected directions is a company that can transform itself to the reality of the changed environment. A company that clings to how it *wishes,* hopes, or erroneously imagines its future environment to be will be uprooted, broken, or at least badly shaken. Successful companies that remain steadfast over time and under widely varying conditions are usually lean. The Lean Management System molds your company so that it has the sensors to see change, the flexibility to accept it, and the resources to survive it.

As an attitude, Delta Zero supports the ultimate purpose of the Lean Management System: growing a blue chip company. This program is not for those wanting to reap quick riches from a source that will disappear with next economic cycle. The Lean Management System is for companies with a commitment to building a source of high and steady income over the long term. It's about building a legacy for the future. Most important, it's about building your own personal commitment to growth.

NOTE

1. *Merriam-Webster's Collegiate Dictionary,* 10th ed. (Springfield, MA: Merriam Webster, 1993).

CHAPTER 3

Steps in Corporate Diagnosis

CORPORATE DIAGNOSIS INVOLVES MANAGERS in a direct, formal inter-action with the employees who are responsible for implementing a compa-ny's annual policy. Diagnosis is not a matter of executive preference; there are no random visits and no pet issues. Rather, the diagnosis is a structured knowledge-gathering and assessment activity based on the company's vision and strategy, its development plan, and its annual policy. Since these guid-ing principles are broadcast throughout the company during deployment of the annual policy, the managers who conduct the diagnosis must work with-in that policy framework.

The diagnosis is a set of steps that are carried out at different organiza-tional levels depending on the size and complexity of the company. Top management in smaller companies may be so familiar with all areas of oper-ation that they can diagnose the entire company's progress toward all its lean management targets in one round. In larger companies, however, the number of work units and targets to review often requires top management to delegate a preliminary round of audits to *diagnostic teams* composed of managers more familiar with daily operations. These diagnostic teams assess progress in the key areas and control points at the work unit level. In the

Lean Management System, the diagnostic teams may be synonymous with the deployment teams that transmitted the annual policy and targets during the strategic improvement cycle. In any case, we suggest a team of around nine members, with twelve an absolute maximum. After the diagnostic teams gather information, top management reviews and interprets the scores, prepares its own follow-up questions, conducts site visits, and then determines overall scores for the company.

This chapter describes the basic diagnostic process for evaluating individual work units, with some reference to the companywide diagnosis in the matter of the questions used. The process of scoring each work unit and developing overall scores for the company is described in Chapter 4.

It is important to remember that the purpose of Corporate Diagnosis is not to judge individual work units as successes or failures. Rather, the point is to monitor the progress of the company as a whole in learning to implement significant changes that support future competitiveness. Work units that score poorly in a particular key should be encouraged, not kicked.

The Corporate Diagnosis audit has four basic stages:

- Preparation
- Site visit to plant or individual work units
- Analysis, scoring, and short-term prescription
- Recognition of achievement

PREPARATION

The preparatory stage of Corporate Diagnosis actually begins with reporting and analysis.* At every level from the shop floor to the boardroom, management teams review regular, ongoing status reports related to the improvement targets they have set for the various lean management keys. In the context of regular reporting and analysis, the Corporate Diagnosis is not a surprise to managers or to the particular unit reviewed.

Getting ready for the actual diagnosis involves two steps:

- Development of questions
- Report from the unit diagnosed

*This takes place during Phase III (Adherence) of the Strategic Improvement Cycle (see Chapter 7 of *Implementing a Lean Management System*).

Development of Questions

The team conducting the diagnosis first generates a set of questions to guide the review that will occur during a site visit to the unit. Using the nine lean management keys as a framework, the diagnostic team compiles questions about company practices and performance that zero in on what it means to be a lean management organization.

At the work unit level, the diagnostic team asks questions to understand the causal links between performance and capabilities. They also inquire about resources needed and solicit feedback for top management to guide the next round of policy making. The following generic questions help frame the big issues for every key area and control point analyzed:

- What problems did you encounter in pursuing the company's annual policy targets for this control point?
- What procedures did you follow to achieve these results?
- What problems do you foresee in the near future?
- When do you expect the next improvements?
- What information or resources will you require to reach higher targets?
- What recommendations does the unit have for company management?

QUESTION PREPARATION AIDS

Specific audit questions should be based on the company's own experience with customers and competitors in their industry. Different markets will have different definitions of "world class"; diagnostic teams must shape their questions carefully to measure things that influence their company's competitiveness. To prime the thinking of the diagnostic team we have provided two sets of references in the appendixes.

Diagnostic Questions and Progress Tables. The charts in Appendix A contain generic Diagnostic Questions for each control point in the Lean Management System. Below each set of questions is a generic Progress Table for the control point that describes symptoms or characteristics observed at each level of development. The Progress Tables are the distillation of our experience with companies pursuing lean management excellence and with various systems for measuring strategic companywide learning and

Lean Management Reference Table

		Cornerstone	Strengths
Key 8	Lean Equipment Management	**Control Point**	8.2 Autonomous Maintenance

Diagnostic Questions

- Does the company maintain optimal equipment conditions by involving machine operators in daily inspection, cleaning, and lubrication of their own machines?
- Are operators learning equipment function and structure, e.g., mechanics, hydraulics, pneumatics, electrical systems, drive systems, etc.?
- Can operators apply this knowledge in conducting daily inspections of their own equipment, in lubricating equipment regularly, and in making occasional basic repairs, replacements, and improvements?

Progress Tables

Level 5 Mass Production	Level 4 System Initiation	Level 3 System Development	Level 2 System Maturity	Level 1 System Excellence

• High functional walls, adversarial relations, and ineffective communication among engineering, maintenance and production personnel
• If any preventive maintenance is carried out, it is performed by maintenance personnel
• Operators "operate" equipment. When it goes down, they expect maintenance to "fix" it. Maintenance has learned not to expect cooperation from production
	• Operator teams are formed to work with maintenance and take responsibility for establishing and maintaining optimal equipment conditions
	• Operators expose and correct equipment abnormalities
	• Steps 1, 2, and 3 of Autonomous Maintenance implemented in pilot areas:
	  1. Initial cleaning
	  2. Identify and eliminate sources of dirt and contamination
	  3. Operators create initial standards for cleaning, inspection, and lubrication
		• Working closely with maintenance engineering personnel, operators learn and understand equipment functions and structure
		• Steps 1, 2, and 3 implemented area- and companywide
		• Step 4 of Autonomous Maintenance implemented in pilot areas:
		  4. Operators are trained to conduct general equipment inspections
			• Operators learn the relation between equipment conditions and quality
			• Step 4 implemented area and companywide
			• Steps 5 and 6 of Autonomous Maintenance implemented in pilot areas:
			  5. Operators conduct general inspections autonomously
			  6. Operators organize and manage equipment and the workplace with the 5S's and visual controls
				• Autonomous Maintenance fully implemented in all areas (step 7)
				• Operator teams incorporate quality maintenance standards into their daily routines
				• Operators participate in ongoing equipment improvement activities with support of engineering and maintenance personnel

FIGURE 3-1.
SAMPLE PROGRESS TABLE FOR THE AUTONOMOUS MAINTENANCE CONTROL POINT

improvement. Together, the Diagnostic Questions and Progress Tables present a picture managers can use to understand the sequence of development and to prepare appropriate questions. Figure 3-1 shows a sample page from these tables for the Autonomous Maintenance control point.

Concordances to Criteria of Major Awards. The Concordances in Appendix B are another resource for drafting diagnosis questions. The Concordances link the lean management keys and control points to the relevant criteria of the world's major productivity and quality awards, as well as to Hiroyuki Hirano's *JIT Implementation Manual* and to Iwao Kobayashi's *20 Keys to Workplace Improvement,* two well-known frameworks for company transformation. Figure 3-2 shows a sample Concordance page for the Lean Equipment Management key.

WHICH KEYS TO CONSIDER

Companywide CEO's Diagnosis. For the companywide diagnosis, the top management team should prepare questions for each of the nine keys. Since this audit often follows a unit-by-unit audit, the questions may be broader than the unit level questions. The top management team should be sure to include questions addressing the firm's strategy, structure, and strengths. (These three categories are indicated at the top of each appendix chart for easy reference.) This will ensure a balanced approach to monitoring important factors in the lean management transformation.

Work Unit Diagnosis. Beyond the general questions listed on p. 29, the diagnostic team will focus on the keys and control points related to the targets assigned to specific work units during deployment of the annual policy. A functional area undergoing review will require a question set that corresponds closely to its role in the company. For example, a production department might emphasize Keys 7 and 8, *lean production* and *lean equipment management.* Because the company's functional structure may not match the structure of the generic sample questions, companies again are encouraged to adapt these questions to their own requirements.

Work unit diagnoses should include also all questions in the keys related to Structure—*lean organization, partnering,* and *information architecture.* These factors are universal. There is no manager in any department or on any team who does not share responsibility for enacting company policies with respect to these keys. In addition, every diagnosis should include questions

Lean Management System	Lean Production Implementation Systems		Criteria of Major Quality and Productivity Awards			
Keys and Control Points	Hirano: JIT Implementation	Kobayashi: 20 Keys	Baldrige Award (ASQC)	Shingo Prize (NAM)	Deming Prize (JUSE)	PM Prize (JIPM)
8. Lean Equipment Management	13. Maintenance and Safety	Key 9. Maintaining Equipment		II.(B) Manufacturing Process Integration		
8.1 Equipment/Process Improvement						2. Focused Improvement
8.2 Autonomous Maintenance					8(6) Instrumentation and inspection	3. Autonomous Maintenance
8.3 Planned Maintenance						4. Planned Maintenance
8.4 Quality Maintenance				II.(C) Quality and Productivity Methods Integration	8(4) Process design, process analysis and process control and improvement	5. Quality Maintenance
8.5 Early Equipment Management						6. Early Product and Equipment Management
8.6 Safety					8(2) Preventive activities for safety and product liability	9. Safety, Hygiene, and Environmental Controls
8.7 Equipment Investment and Maintenance Prevention Design						6(6); 6(7) [MP design and feedback systems] 6(8) [equipment economics and risk analysis] 6(9) [equipment budget]

FIGURE 3-2.
SAMPLE CONCORDANCE FOR LEAN EQUIPMENT MANAGEMENT

about Key 6, *culture of improvement,* and its control points—standardization, waste-free strategy, technology diffusion, and education. These items are critical because they indicate how well the company learns and grows in response to daily challenges and chronic problems. Review of these items should not be relegated to the overall company diagnosis alone.

In many work unit audits, the questions related to Strategy will not be required. There are important exceptions, however. For example, independently from the companywide diagnosis, the top management team may give *itself* a work unit audit on the entire strategic planning and deployment system. All the Strategy questions should be answered each time the planning system itself is diagnosed—at least once a year. Answers to the Strategy questions indicate to what extent the company is a learning organization relative to its global competition.

Important strategic initiatives also require strong formal links to the strategic planning process. Thus, Strategy questions should be included as part of the production department's diagnosis during any major change program, for example

- when diagnosing quality assurance capabilities during a TQM implementation
- when diagnosing production capabilities during a JIT implementation
- when diagnosing asset management capabilities during a TPM implementation

SCHEDULING THE DIAGNOSIS

Corporate Diagnosis is not a "pop quiz" sprung on unsuspecting unit managers and employees during a surprise visit. Rather, it is a milestone in a mutual learning process. The unit to be reviewed should be notified several weeks before the proposed site visit. The diagnostic team should submit its questions and site visit agenda at that time, so unit managers and employees have plenty of time to prepare.

Report from the Unit Diagnosed

In response to the diagnostic questions, the employees and managers of the unit prepare a special report that addresses the questions. The report tells what the unit has done to carry out key-related activities in the previous improvement cycle, and also describes results and why they do or don't meet the assigned targets. (In some companies, this pre-visit report may be an application from the work unit for official certification to the next higher level of achievement in particular key areas.) The diagnostic team reviews the work unit report in preparation for the site visit.

The pre-visit report must be short , concrete, and to the point, with no more than two pages per hour of scheduled site visit. Brevity promotes useful interaction between the diagnostic team and the individuals and teams in the work unit. Long-winded reports that leave no question unanswered will leave unit employees little to discuss with the diagnostic team.

THE DIAGNOSTIC SITE VISIT

The site visit is the plant's or unit's chance to show management its daily operating conditions—and management's opportunity to observe, ask more specific questions, and note ideas that can be implemented more broadly. During a site visit, the diagnostic team has an opportunity to see firsthand what the unit has accomplished in the key areas and control points of lean management. Usually a full day is scheduled to visit an entire plant. If the unit diagnosed is a department or a work area, the visit may be shorter. The diagnostic team determines the length of the visit and prepares an agenda, after considering the ground to be covered and the depth of questioning to be pursued.

Preparing the Diagnostic Form

Before the site visit, the diagnostic team prepares a Diagnostic Form for each control point examined during the audit. A blank version of this form is shown in Figure 3-3. At the top of the Diagnostic Form, team members enter the relevant lean management cornerstone (strategy, structure, or strengths), then the key, control point, and checkpoint examined. They identify the work unit and the members of the diagnostic team, followed by a summary of the diagnostic questions they have prepared for the unit. Figure 3-4 shows the Diagnostic Form with questions filled in for the Autonomous Maintenance control point. The bottom of the Diagnostic Form is a space for notes, in a five-column format similar to that of the

Diagnostic Form

	Cornerstone
Key	Control Point
Checkpoint	
Unit Diagnosed	Date
Diagnostic Team	

Diagnostic Questions

Notes

Level 5 Mass Production	Level 4 System Initiation	Level 3 System Development	Level 2 System Maturity	Level 1 System Excellence

FIGURE 3-3.
BLANK DIAGNOSTIC FORM

Diagnostic Form

		Cornerstone	Strengths
Key	8. Lean Equipment Management	**Control Point**	8.2 Autonomous Maintenance
Checkpoint	Steps 1–3: Initial cleaning, elimination of sources of dirt, establishment of inspection standards		
Unit Diagnosed	Production Area A	**Date**	10/7/1996
Diagnostic Team	Lean Equipment Management Initiative Deployment Team		

Diagnostic Questions	
• Is everyone on the team involved in Autonomous Maintenance activities? • Have all team members completed introductory training about their role in preventing equipment breakdown? • Step 1: Has the team completed the initial cleaning for all equipment in the workplace?	• Step2: Has the team taken steps to eliminate source of dirt and make it easier to maintain basic conditions? • Step 3: Has the team established a set of initial standards for regular equipment inspection and put them in checklist form? • Has the team satisfactorily passed the supervisor's audits for each of these three steps?

Notes

Level 5 Mass Production	Level 4 System Initiation	Level 3 System Development	Level 2 System Maturity	Level 1 System Excellence

FIGURE 3-4.
SAMPLE DIAGNOSTIC FORM SHOWING QUESTIONS FOR AUTONOMOUS MAINTENANCE CONTROL POINT

Progress Tables. For the site visit, diagnostic team members carry copies of the form on clipboards as a reference and a place to record and organize their observations.

The site visit often begins with a tour of the unit to show innovations since the last review—and in world class companies, the employees do more of the talking than their unit managers. Many site visits also involve observing the visual controls that the unit uses for daily work management and reporting; an example is the Workcenter Control Board described in *Implementing a Lean Management System*. Team leaders and unit managers must be prepared to exhibit whatever data is necessary to strengthen their answers or arguments in response to the diagnostic questions.

The point of the site visit is to highlight problems in systems and processes and to identify non-value-adding wastes. Diagnosis should help people recognize gaps between goals and performance and encourage improvement. In this light, diagnostic teams should be careful to avoid laying blame.

As they tour the workplace and hear presentations, members of the diagnostic team listen and observe carefully. To focus their thinking, they bring along a prepared scoring aid such as the Question and Progress Table sheets from Appendix A. In a certification-oriented system, the diagnostic team would also bring a checklist of required criteria for each level.

Recording Observations

The diagnostic team takes careful notes on the Diagnostic Form to support later discussion and scoring. To organize their notes, team members refer to the Diagnostic Question/Progress Table page for the control point they are auditing. They consider the symptoms or characteristics described in the chart for each level of development, relative to what they are seeing and hearing in the unit, and then enter their observations in the corresponding columns on the Diagnostic Form. Figure 3-5 shows the Diagnostic Form for Autonomous Maintenance as it might appear after the audit, with notes on the points mentioned in the Progress Table that was shown in Figure 3-1. The completed form provides a record of observation that supports the post-audit discussion in which scores are determined.

Diagnostic Form

		Cornerstone	Strengths
Key	8. Lean Equipment Management	**Control Point**	8.2 Autonomous Maintenance
Checkpoint	Steps 1–3: Initial cleaning, elimination of sources of dirt, establishment of inspection standards		
Unit Diagnosed	Production Area A	**Date**	10/7/1996
Diagnostic Team	Lean Equipment Management Initiative Deployment Team		

Diagnostic Questions

- Is everyone on the team involved in Autonomous Maintenance activities?
- Have all team members completed introductory training about their role in preventing equipment breakdown?
- Step 1: Has the team completed the initial cleaning for all equipment in the workplace?

- Step2: Has the team taken steps to eliminate source of dirt and make it easier to maintain basic conditions?
- Step 3: Has the team established a set of initial standards for regular equipment inspection and put them in checklist form?
- Has the team satisfactorily passed the supervisor's audits for each of these three steps?

Notes

Level 5 Mass Production	Level 4 System Initiation	Level 3 System Development	Level 2 System Maturity	Level 1 System Excellence
	Operator teams are formed for Autonomous Maintenance activities in pilot areas; *Operators are trained to recognize abnormalities in their equipment.* *A checklist of initial standards has been created and is used in daily inspections (Autonomous Maintenance Step 3).* *The team has passed the supervisor's audits Step 1 and Step 2. Getting ready for audits on Step 3.*	*Steps 1 and 2 deployed areawide. Team leaders from pilot areas are helping train new teams.*		

FIGURE 3-5.
SAMPLE DIAGNOSTIC FORM SHOWING OBSERVATIONS FOR AUTONOMOUS MAINTENANCE CONTROL POINT

ANALYSIS, SCORING, AND SHORT-TERM PRESCRIPTION

Immediately after the site visit, the diagnostic team meets with department heads and area managers in a conference room to determine scores for the unit. Our experience suggests that using a round or square table—one that has no "head"—helps take the discussion outside a bureaucratic framework and promotes teamwork and open dialogue. The group reviews what they have observed and discusses what score to give. If the answer is not obvious from comparing their notes to the Progress Tables, they may apply a more universal set of criteria from the Diagnostic Scoring Matrix (Figure 4-2, described in the next chapter). It should be emphasized that scores are reached by a process of qualified consensus. Team members do not have to agree unanimously on the score, but must be willing to support the score that is reached.

After determining a score for the unit, the diagnostic team and unit manager review the picture of unit conditions that has emerged. Stressing positive results and achievements, they identify improvement areas, offer implementation insights, and prescribe short-term actions and further research or training if necessary. The reviewers summarize their observations and prepare a report for the unit as well as for upper management. The diagnosed unit develops action plans for each performance gap or weak area identified. Immediate action is taken where appropriate. The team submits any long-term recommendations for the unit to the top management team to become a part of the next year's improvement policy.

RECOGNITION OF ACHIEVEMENT

After all units have been diagnosed and the companywide diagnosis has been completed, hold an informal meeting, such as a reception or dinner party, to celebrate progress. This celebration recognizes the hard work of the previous year and brings together the various teams, units, and departments as one company working on a set of integrated goals.

Key Points in Work Unit Diagnosis

- Don't just check results. Evaluate the *process* through which the results were obtained.
- During the audit, discrepancies may appear among different data. In such cases, the diagnostic team should concentrate on the problem and seek its causes. Avoid looking for culprits to blame.
- Review visual information showing the activities carried out. Diagrams, control charts, and similar graphic materials are very helpful for communicating, clarifying and confirming information.
- Allow sufficient time for discussion so that information can be communicated and processed effectively.

CHAPTER 4

Diagnostic Scoring

THIS CHAPTER EXPLAINS HOW TO SCORE each part of the firm on the keys and control points covered by the lean management diagnostic system, and how to develop overall scores for the company. The purpose of scoring is to rate the unit and the firm objectively in each of the nine keys and to gain a better understanding of the complex technical and human factors that may affect performance in each control point. Past efforts should be recognized, but as the word "diagnosis" suggests, the intention of scoring is to point the direction for corrective action and future improvements. The level assigned should reflect the organization's achievements and, more important, the challenges it faces internally and externally. So it is wise to err on the side of strict application. Diagnosis should lead to a proactive strategic response. It is pointless to pat oneself on the back.

USING THE PROGRESS TABLES FOR SCORING

To aid diagnostic scoring, the lean management Progress Tables in Appendix A help managers understand what to look for in the nine lean management keys and their control points. For each control point, these tables express the criteria as concrete symptoms or results, arranged according to the five levels of organizational learning. In effect, this is a road map for lean management development that helps the company know its position.

As Chapter 3 described, the diagnostic team refers to the Progress Tables as it develops questions, tours the work unit, and receives responses to its questions. Sometimes scoring a work unit's development in a particular control point is a simple matter of locating the observed symptoms on the table and reading the level from that. Often, however, the symptoms don't fall clearly within one level. Since the point of diagnosis is to uncover gaps and to simultaneously develop interrelated systems, the general rule is to score the unit at the lower level of development rather than building a falsely elevated picture of the company's capabilities. Figure 4-1 illustrates this with the Diagnostic Form and Progress Table from the previous chapter. The diagnosed unit has fulfilled all the requirements for level 4 in autonomous maintenance, but only one of the level 3 requirements; it should be scored a 4. Averaging the scores of the symptoms at the unit level could give an unrealistic picture of the unit's actual development. Be especially wary of situations where world class results are not supported by development of world class systems that will make the results sustainable.

USING THE SCORING CRITERIA

When it is unclear how to score a unit for a particular control point, the diagnostic team may resort to a more abstract analysis of the symptoms. This analysis uses four Scoring Criteria—*Reliable Method, Extent of Deployment, Extent of Cross-Functional Integration,* and *Results.* These criteria are the principles from which the Progress Tables were developed. The Scoring Criteria can be summarized in four basic questions:

- *Reliable method:* Does the firm adopt a systematic approach to identifying and deploying best practices?
- *Extent of deployment:* How well is the practice deployed throughout the company?
- *Extent of cross-functional integration:* How well is the practice integrated across functional lines?
- *Results:* Of what significance are the results achieved?

Lean Management Reference Table		Cornerstone	Strengths
Key 8	Lean Equipment Management	Control Point	8.2 Autonomous Maintenance

Diagnostic Questions

- Does the company maintain optimal equipment conditions by involving machine operators in daily inspection, cleaning, and lubrication of their own machines?
- Are operators learning equipment function and structure, e.g., mechanics, hydraulics, pneumatics, electrical systems, drive systems, etc.?
- Can operators apply this knowledge in conducting daily inspections of their own equipment, in lubricating equipment regularly, and in making occasional basic repairs, replacements, and improvements?

Progress Tables

Level 5 Mass Production	Level 4 System Initiation	Level 3 System Development	Level 2 System Maturity	Level 1 System Excellence

• High functional walls, adversarial relations, and ineffective communication among engineering, maintenance and production personnel
• If any preventive maintenance is carried out, it is performed by maintenance personnel
• Operators "operate" equipment. When it goes down, they expect maintenance to "fix" it. Maintenance has learned not to expect cooperation from production
	Operator teams are formed to work with maintenance and take responsibility for establishing and maintaining optimal equipment conditions
	• Operators expose and correct equipment abnormalities
	• Steps 1, 2, and 3 of Autonomous Maintenance implemented in pilot areas:
	  1. Initial cleaning
	  2. Identify and eliminate sources of dirt and contamination
	  3. Operators create initial standards for cleaning, inspection, and lubrication
		• Working closely with maintenance engineering personnel, operators learn and understand equipment functions and structure
		• Steps 1, 2, and 3 implemented area- and companywide
		Step 4 of Autonomous Maintenance implemented in pilot areas:
		  4. Operators are trained to conduct general equipment inspections
			• Operators learn the relation between equipment conditions and quality
			• Step 4 implemented area and companywide
			• Steps 5 and 6 of Autonomous Maintenance implemented in pilot areas:
			  5. Operators conduct general inspections autonomously
			  6. Operators organize and manage equipment and the workplace with the 5S's and visual controls
				• Autonomous Maintenance fully implemented in all areas (step 7)
				• Operator teams incorporate quality maintenance standards into their daily routines
				• Operators participate in ongoing equipment improvement activities with support of engineering and maintenance personnel

Diagnostic Form		Cornerstone	Strengths
Key	8. Lean Equipment Management	Control Point	8.2 Autonomous Maintenance
Checkpoint	Steps 1–3: Initial cleaning, elimination of sources of dirt, establishment of inspection standards		
Unit Diagnosed	Production Area A	Date	10/7/1996
Diagnostic Team	Lean Equipment Management Initiative Deployment Team		

Diagnostic Questions

- Is everyone on the team involved in Autonomous Maintenance activities?
- Have all team members completed introductory training about their role in preventing equipment breakdown?
- Step 1: Has the team completed the initial cleaning for all equipment in the workplace?

- Step2: Has the team taken steps to eliminate source of dirt and make it easier to maintain basic conditions?
- Step 3: Has the team established a set of initial standards for regular equipment inspection and put them in checklist form?
- Has the team satisfactorily passed the supervisor's audits for each of these three steps?

Notes

Level 5 Mass Production	Level 4 System Initiation	Level 3 System Development	Level 2 System Maturity	Level 1 System Excellence
	Operator teams are formed for Autonomous Maintenance activities in pilot areas. *Operators are trained to recognize abnormalities in their equipment.* *A checklist of initial standards has been created and is used in daily inspections (Autonomous Maintenance Step 3).* *The team has passed the supervisor's audits Step 1 and Step 2. Getting ready for audits on Step 3.*	*Steps 1 and 2 deployed areawide. Team leaders from pilot areas are helping train new teams.*		

FIGURE 4-1.

SCORING FROM THE LEAN MANAGEMENT PROGRESS TABLES

Generally the Progress Tables are more useful during the site visit, but the Scoring Criteria can clarify issues during the post-visit scoring discussion. The criteria are helpful for the companywide diagnosis as well as for the unit audits, since companywide scoring usually entails meshing of individual unit scores, which can vary widely. In reviewing individual work unit performance, diagnostic teams will tend to focus on the first and fourth factors—methods and results. The middle factors, related to deployment and cross-functional integration, while significant in assessing areawide deployment, require a look at the company as a whole. In companywide scoring, the CEO and top management team look at all four factors to determine a score for each key. In cases of imbalance, the diagnostic team should give a lower score (the higher-numbered level). This is particularly important where apparently good results are not supported by well-developed, deployed, and integrated systems.

The following sections define each criterion and give general questions that help the diagnostic team apply it correctly.

Reliable Method

The Reliable Method criterion relates to the improvement methods a company implements to accomplish its objectives. A method is an organizational structure or process used to facilitate or carry out activities like strategic planning, cross-functional coordination, production, and training.

Companies that are considered "world class" reach that status in part by developing and implementing reliable improvement methods that are *best practices*—efficient and continuously improving systems for giving internal and external customers what they need. Best practices include familiar improvement methodologies such as just-in-time, total quality management, total productive maintenance strategies, quick changeover technologies, mistake-proofing, and visual information sharing. Generally speaking, these systems and methods are embodied in the Lean Management System's nine keys to development and are brought out in the diagnostic questions for the various keys. Many top companies have adapted these approaches or created new approaches that give them reliable results. Process benchmarking is therefore an important element in custom-fitting the diagnostic system to a particular company or industry.

In applying this criterion, the diagnostic team should ask several questions of a general nature:

- Is the method used to develop a given key a "best practice"?
- Is the method standardized?
- Is it systematic?
- Can improvement results be replicated?
- Is it prevention-based?
- Is the method or process self-repeating, i.e., capable of generating continuous system improvements?

Extent of Deployment

The Deployment criterion addresses the way the company has deployed the improvement method in question. Extent of Deployment reflects how thoroughly a company documents and replicates or adapts best practices within the company. Scoring questions include the following:

- How pervasive is the method within the company?
- Is it clear what types of lateral deployment are appropriate?
- Is the method replicated wherever appropriate?
- Where direct replication is not appropriate, has the basic principle been applied fully in other areas?

Extent of Cross-Functional Integration

The Cross-Functional Integration criterion looks at how the company coordinates the activities of different divisions, departments, and teams to employ a method. Ideally, improvement activities should be managed cross-functionally using a top-down, bottom-up approach. Cross-functional management is critical to ensure that the right improvement methods, once employed, are sustained and spread throughout a company. Without cross-functional cooperation, a company will fail to become a lean producer, despite initial successes in pilot areas. Scoring questions on Cross-Functional Integration include the following:

- How well is a given method or activity integrated with other activities of the company?

• How effectively is the activity managed across functional lines?

• Has the company eliminated all "disconnects" and "misconnects"?*

Results

Finally, the work units and the company as a whole are scored on the extent to which efforts to improve the key or control point approach world class levels. Scoring questions include the following:

• Are appropriate performance measures in place? Or is evidence anecdotal?

• Does feedback indicate positive results in areas in which the method is employed?

• Is it clear that the positive results are caused by the method?

• How long have such positive trends been sustained?

• Is there evidence that the company can sustain or improve such results in the future?

THE DIAGNOSTIC SCORING MATRIX

For each specific question in the four Scoring Criteria, there is an array of responses. To help diagnostic teams organize their scoring discussion, we have put generic responses to these questions into a scoring aid—the Diagnostic Scoring Matrix (see Figure 4-2). Milestones for each scoring criterion correspond with the five levels of organizational learning of the Lean Management System.

REACHING A COMPANYWIDE SCORE

The diagnostic team proceeds key by key, using Progress Tables and the Diagnostic Scoring System as guidelines in determining the level for each individual control point. The general rule is to score conservatively—it is better to score weakly and in large companies that conduct Corporate

---

*A *disconnect* is an established exchange of materials, personnel, or information between departments or functional units that is required for the method to function effectively, but which has broken down for some reason. A *misconnect* is an exchange between departments or units or individuals that is required for the method to function, but which has never existed or has been improperly designed.

Diagnostic Scoring Matrix

Diagnostic Criteria	Level 5 Mass Production	Level 4 System Initiation	Level 3 System Development	Level 2 System Maturity	Level 1 System Excellence
Reliable Method	• no sytem • poor standards • poor feedback	• new system • some standardization • good basic awareness	• sound system • good standardization with replicable results • some system improvements	• refined PDCA system • excellent standardization • active system improvement	• refined sytem • continuous system improvements
Extent of Deployment	• no awareness • no training • no experimentation	• focused deployment • initial training conducted • pilot projects in major areas	• horizontal deployment –most major areas –some support areas	• full implementation –all major areas –many support areas	• total implementation –all major areas –all support areas –all operations
Extent of Cross-Functional Integration	• haphazard • many misconnects • many disconnects	• conceptualized but not practiced • misconnects and disconnects identified	• practiced but still ad hoc • efforts are made to eliminate misconnects and disconnects	• good integration • very few misconnects and disconnects	• excellent integration • misconnects and disconnects have been eliminated
Results	• well below industry par • no systematic measurement • anecdotal evidence	• below industry par • targets and measures established • positive trends	• on par with industry • positive trends in most major areas	• above industry par • good to excellent in major areas • positive trends in support areas	• best in class • world class in major areas • good to excellent in support areas

FIGURE 4-2.
DIAGNOSTIC SCORING MATRIX

Diagnosis in each work unit, the top management team conducts a separate companywide diagnosis and site visits based on what was learned at the unit level. After reviewing the unit scores for the various control points, the CEO and top managers then discuss what the companywide scores should be. Scoring conservatively to avoid an inflated view of the situation, the top management team works to reach a qualified consensus just as the midlevel management teams did following their site visits (see Chapter 3). Ultimately, they arrive at one score for each of the company's control points.

The Lean Management Scoreboard

The Lean Management Scoreboard is a form for displaying the company's scores in all the control points; it guides companywide scoring by making it easy to calculate average scores for each key. Figure 4-3 is a sample scoreboard showing the results of a diagnosis conducted by the Nonesuch Casting Company, a composite company introduced as a running example in *Implementing a Lean Management System*.

The diagnostic team reaches a tentative score for each key by calculating the unweighted average score for the control points listed under that key. An unweighted average is used to emphasize that each control point is an integral part of a subsystem of lean management. For example, to calculate Nonesuch Casting's unweighted average score for the *lean equipment management* key, the team adds the points of the seven scores for the individual control points, then divides by 7:

$$\frac{4 + 5 + 3 + 4 + 5 + 3 + 4}{7} = 4$$

The average score for each key is entered in the boxes on the right side of the Lean Management Scoreboard.

It is important to remember that scoring is an analytical activity that requires more than simple averaging. Managers must look carefully at the scores they are averaging. If the company scores a 5 in one control point and a 1 in another, for example, scoring it a 3 may not be useful.

The final scores determined by the top management team will be plotted as a baseline or a development update on the company's five-year Development Plan. Figure 4-4 shows the Nonesuch Casting Development

CORNER-STONES OF GROWTH	KEYS TO DEVELOPMENT	CONTROL POINTS	5 Levels of Organizational Learning					
			Level 5	Level 4	Level 3	Level 2	Level 1	
Strategy	1 Customer focus	1.1 Customer requirements				✔		
		1.2 Customer relationships				✔		$\frac{6}{3} = \boxed{2}$
		1.3 Order-to-delivery process				✔		
	2 Leadership	2.1 Business renewal		✔				
		2.2 Focus		✔				
		2.3 Standardization		✔				$\frac{20}{5} = \boxed{4}$
		2.4 Adherence		✔				
		2.5 Reflection		✔				
Structure	3 Lean organization	3.1 Team activities			✔			
		3.2 Networked organization			✔			
		3.3 Rewards + recognition			✔			$\frac{15}{5} = \boxed{3}$
		3.4 Evaluation + compensation		✔				
		3.5 Lean administration				✔		
	4 Partnering	4.1 Employee value		✔				
		4.2 Comakership			✔			$\frac{12}{4} = \boxed{3}$
		4.3 Environmental impact			✔			
		4.4 Social integrity			✔			
	5 Information architecture	5.1 Workplace org. & vis. control		✔				
		5.2 Fast feedback systems				✔		$\frac{12}{4} = \boxed{3}$
		5.3 Performance measurement				✔		
		5.4 Kaizen reporting		✔				
Strengths	6 Culture of improvement	6.1 Standardization	✔					
		6.2 Waste-free strategy		✔				$\frac{16}{4} = \boxed{4}$
		6.3 Technology diffusion	✔					
		6.4 Education			✔			
	7 Lean production	7.1 Flow production			✔			
		7.2 Multiprocess handling	✔					
		7.3 Leveled, mixed model prod.		✔				
		7.4 Quick changeover		✔				$\frac{28}{7} = \boxed{4}$
		7.5 Automation with a human touch	✔					
		7.6 Pull system/coupled production			✔			
		7.7 Production scheduling		✔				
	8 Lean equipment management	8.1 Equip./process improvement		✔				
		8.2 Autonomous maintenance	✔					
		8.3 Planned maintenance			✔			
		8.4 Quality maintenance		✔				$\frac{28}{7} = \boxed{4}$
		8.5 Early equipment management	✔					
		8.6 Safety			✔			
		8.7 Equip. invest./maint. prev. design		✔				
	9 Lean engineering	9.1 Design process				✔		$\frac{4}{2} = \boxed{2}$
		9.2 Design for QCD				✔		

FIGURE 4-3.
LEAN MANAGEMENT SCOREBOARD

		5 Levels of Organizational Learning				
Corner-stones of Growth	Keys to Development	Level 5	Level 4	Level 3	Level 2	Level 1
		Mass production	System initiation	System development	System maturity	System excellence
Strategy	1 Customer focus				Base-line Year 1 Year 3	Year 5
	2 Leadership		Base-line	Year 1 Year 3	Year 5	
Structure	3 Lean organization			Base-line Year 1 Year 3	Year 5	
	4 Partnering			Base-line Year 1 Year 3	Year 5	
	5 Information architecture			Base-line Year 1 Year 3	Year 5	
Strengths	6 Culture of improvement			Base-line Year 1 Year 3	Year 5	
	7 Lean production		Base-line	Year 1 Year 3	Year 5	
	8 Lean equipment management		Base-line	Year 1	Year 3 Year 5	
	9 Lean engineering				Base-line Year 1 Year 3	Year 5

FIGURE 4-4.
DEVELOPMENT PLAN AFTER YEAR 1 DIAGNOSIS

Plan after the first year of improvement activities, inserting scores for "Year 1" in between the baseline and the "Year 3" goals. (The company has highlighted Keys 1 and 9 as strategic keys for long-term development and is supporting them by strengthening its other keys.)

The Lean Radar Chart

The Lean Radar Chart is another useful tool for visualizing company-wide progress in the nine keys. This is a target-like image with nine spokes representing the nine keys. After scoring the company, the top management team enters the score for each key at the intersection of the appropriate spoke and development level, then connects the dots to make a polygon. After each successive diagnosis, the company's scores are displayed with another color. Where the company has progressed to the next level, the chart shows new lines inside the old ones. Keys that have not improved appear clearly as overlaps of the old score. Figure 4-5 shows Lean Radar Charts created for Nonesuch Casting from its baseline diagnosis and from the diagnosis at the end of Year 1. Posted throughout the company's facilities, radar charts provide important feedback, reminding employees and managers of the company's lean management status and inspiring continuous improvement in every part of the organization.

After Baseline Diagnosis

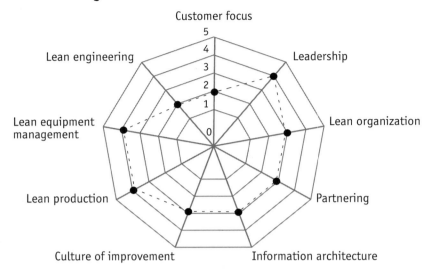

After Year 1 Diagnosis

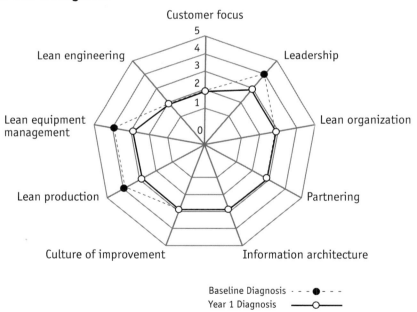

Baseline Diagnosis · – – ● – – ·
Year 1 Diagnosis ——○——

FIGURE 4-5.
LEAN RADAR CHARTS

Diagnostic Questions and Lean Management Progress Tables

THE FOLLOWING REFERENCE TABLES combine generic Diagnostic Questions for the control points of the Lean Management System with Progress Tables that present the characteristics observed in companies at each level of organizational learning. Developed from our experience with numerous companies and with world class criteria for various aspects of lean management, these tables will be useful in developing company-specific diagnostic questions. They are also helpful as scoring aids during the site visit, particularly when used with the Diagnostic Form shown in Figure 3-3 (p. 35). Figure 4-1 on p. 43 gives an example of how to use the reference charts and the Diagnostic Form together to record notes and determine the score.

Lean Management Reference Table

		Cornerstone	Strategy
Key 1	Customer Focus	**Control Point**	1.1 Customer Requirements

Diagnostic Questions

- Does the company have a "market-in" orientation, e.g., does the company use customer feedback to define quality, cost, and delivery requirements?
- Does the company systematically collect and analyze information about customer satisfaction?
- Does the company systematically anticipate what will delight the customer?

Progress Tables

Level 5 Mass Production	Level 4 System Initiation	Level 3 System Development	Level 2 System Maturity	Level 1 System Excellence
• No established quality policy or system; quality defined as whatever sells • No systematic measure of customer satisfaction • Product-out orientation • Customer complaints are ignored; those who complain are "guilty until proven innocent" • No records of customer feedback are kept • Failure to meet customer requirements	• Basic quality system established on paper; quality defined as whatever is not returned • Company can pass an ISO 9000 paper audit • Measure of customer satisfaction based on expressed requirements only • Customers cultivated as primary information source on quality, cost, delivery, performance • Still periodically fails to meet customer requirements	• Quality system has been deployed; company complies with own system; quality is defined by AQL • Company can pass both paper and on-site ISO 9000 audits • Measure of customer satisfaction based on unexpressed as well as expressed requirements • System established for gathering information from customers • Customer information drives continuous improvement of quality, cost, delivery • Customer's expressed requirements met, but unexpressed requirements still unmet	• Quality system being refined, but still defined by AQL • Measure of customer satisfaction based on expressed, unexpressed, and latent requirements • Expressed, unexpressed requirements met, but failure in delighting customer • System for gathering information standardized and fully deployed • Efforts underway to increase flexibility and speed of response at every level	• Quality system being refined; quality is defined as Zero Defects • Measure of customer satisfaction based on expressed, unexpressed, and latent requirements • In all systems, standard operation and continuous improvement defined by customer requirements • Reputation as customer-oriented supplier of quality products firmly established • Firm regularly delights customer by anticipating latent requirements

Lean Management Reference Table

		Cornerstone	Strategy
Key 1	Customer Focus	**Control Point**	1.2 Customer Relationships

Diagnostic Questions

- Has the company established effective procedures to gather and use information from customers to improve quality, cost, and delivery?
- Has the company established effective procedures to systematically monitor customer satisfaction?
- Is a system in place for obtaining customer feedback and relaying it to the design team?
- Are employees empowered to anticipate customer needs and take corrective action?

Progress Tables

Level 5 Mass Production	Level 4 System Initiation	Level 3 System Development	Level 2 System Maturity	Level 1 System Excellence
• The firm has no system for managing customer relationships • Orientation to the market is product-out; customers are assumed to be interested in price, not quality and service	• Orientation is still product-out, but top management initiates TQM as its approach to the customer, who is seen to be interested in cost, quality, delivery, and service	• Strong relationships with customers have been established and there is a market-in orientation • After-sales service supports customer enjoyment of product and identifies mismatches between design and customer need • Employees throughout the company are empowered to have contact with buyers and to take appropriate corrective action	• Market-in approach emphasizes service elements of all products • Feedback from service in the field to design teams ensures better match between design and need	• Customer relationships are strong; there is a refined system of interaction and feedback • Customer needs are anticipated • After-sales service ensures customer delight

Lean Management Reference Table

	Cornerstone	Strategy
Key 1 Customer Focus	**Control Point**	1.3 Order-to-Delivery Process

Diagnostic Questions

- Has the company eliminated waste and ineffectiveness within and between all parts of the value chain, from design to manufacturing, distribution, and after-sales service?
- Have indirect areas such as administration, accounting, marketing, sales, and finance been included in process improvement?

Progress Tables

Level 5 Mass Production	Level 4 System Initiation	Level 3 System Development	Level 2 System Maturity	Level 1 System Excellence
• No understanding of the relationship between process waste and customer satisfaction • No recognition of the need to analyze and engineer the processes in the value chain	• Begin to implement the Lean Management System • Analyze total business, entire value chain from design to manufacturing, to identified non-value-added waste	• Performance measures throughout the company are geared to key process indicators of customer satisfaction, e.g., Lean Production System measures	• Fast feedback systems catch errors, prevent defects, and shorten reaction times between discovery of errors and process abnormalities and corrective action	• Total business is engineered to serve the customer by delivering the products customers want, when they want them, without waste

Lean Management Reference Table

	Cornerstone	Strategy
Key 2	Leadership	
	Control Point	2.1 Business Renewal

Diagnostic Questions

- Does the company cultivate a clear and creative vision of the future of the business in a disciplined and open way?
- Has the company communicated that vision to all employees in a succinct and motivating statement?
- Does the company carefully probe the nature of its core capabilities, processes, and key factors for success?
- Has the company leveraged existing capabilities and resources to be sure it will have a competitive portfolio of capabilities in the future?

- Has the company made its long-term strategy concrete by making long- and medium-term development plans?
- Is the company prepared to change its strategic direction and realign its people and resources if necessary?

Progress Tables

Level 5 Mass Production	Level 4 System Initiation	Level 3 System Development	Level 2 System Maturity	Level 1 System Excellence
• Company leadership models the future unsystematically • Generally does not expect change in vision; oriented to single model • Limited knowledge of core capabilities • No long-range plans	• Top management begins modeling "what-if" scenarios • Begins studying core capabilities • Gathers information for strategic analysis that can support 3- to 5-year policies, but— • Policies are not clear and resulting plans are not streamlined	• Top management constructs alternative scenarios, anticipates change, plans strategic response • Understands capabilities and fit with market • Constructs strategies and 3- to 5-year plans based on research and modeling • Basic targets and means are clear, but analysis of the work environment may be weak	• Management expands change-scenario inputs to fine-tune strategic alternatives (computer modeling a viable option) • Easily assimilates new methods and technologies • Benchmarking shows company well beyond average within industry • Strategy and 3- to 5-year plans are consistent, but linking mid- to long-range plans and annual policies is weak	• Management uses modeling efficiently and regularly • Company in tune with capabilities and leads industry • Clear, continuous links between strategy, mid- to long-range plans and policy, supported by understanding and adherence to PDCA cycles

Lean Management Reference Table

	Cornerstone	Strategy
Key 2	Leadership	
	Control Point	2.2 Focus

Diagnostic Questions

- Does the company and its top management team systematically redefine its strategy to align individuals, systems, and resources to the conditions of the market and the competitive environment?
- Has the company established effective procedures for analyzing data on improvement goals achievement?
- Can the top management team effectively identify and focus companywide attention of critical areas for improvement?
- Are all areas of strategic planning integrated, e.g., policy and budget control?

Progress Tables

Level 5 Mass Production	Level 4 System Initiation	Level 3 System Development	Level 2 System Maturity	Level 1 System Excellence
• Improvement initiatives not linked to strategy or based on thorough regular companywide diagnosis and analysis • Plans are not process-focused	• Diagnosis of past year results in some clear policies, but— • Analysis and isolation of critical problems and factors is weak • Weak correlation of targets and means • Budgets planned separately	• Annual diagnosis now focuses on critical problems • Integration of policy development and budgeting is planned • Development of targets and means is based on cause and effect analysis, but— • Problem-solving skills are weak • Policy and planning are still viewed as formalities; links between plans at different levels are weak	• Annual diagnosis is supported and refined by effective kaizen reporting at lower levels • Policy plans are directed at critical problems • Links between plans at different levels are clear • Still budget-control oriented; weak profit plan	• Procedures for annual diagnosis are standardized and fully followed • Emphasis is on improvement and breakthrough well-linked to budget control • Plan adjustments are easy to discern when required and implemented quickly

Lean Management Reference Table

		Cornerstone	Strategy
Key 2	Leadership	**Control Point**	2.3 Standardization

Diagnostic Questions

- Has the company established effective procedures to communicate or deploy its policies effectively to all managers, team leaders, and supervisors who have responsibility for policy implementation?
- Has the company developed a control system that clearly links company policy with departmental goals and daily work (vertical deployment)?
- Has the company developed a system and organized its teams to support cross-functional integration and management of company policy targets (horizontal deployment)?
- Is there a clear relation between daily work and the policy targets and means?
- How deeply are teams, small groups, and individuals involved in establishing their own goals?

Progress Tables

Level 5 Mass Production	Level 4 System Initiation	Level 3 System Development	Level 2 System Maturity	Level 1 System Excellence
• Plans to implement company policy and progress control are haphazard • No coordination of improvement activities occurs between different levels of the organization • Efforts are inconsistent and incomplete	• Preliminary efforts at vertical and horizontal deployment and coordination of plans are undertaken, but— • Links between team activities at various levels and management policy targets are weak	• Policy plans and useful measures extend to the floor level and reflect thorough analysis of previous year, but— • Horizontal coordination of plans and control indicators is weak (between related departments)	• Good coordination horizontally and vertically, but— • Coordination and deployment are not systematic (procedures not standardized) • Team targets are linked with company goals, but team members are not consistently involved in setting them or establishing individual goals	• Standardized, step-by-step procedures for coordination of plans are in place and followed • Deployment is consistent at all levels • Team and individual goals reflect clear understanding of company goals

Lean Management Reference Table

		Cornerstone	Strategy
Key 2	Leadership	**Control Point**	2.4 Adherence

Diagnostic Questions

- Is the annual policy managed visually, so that everyone in the company can see policy targets, responsibilities, schedules, progress, and problems at a glance?
- Does the reporting system support cross-functional management?
- How deeply are teams, small groups, and individuals involved in evaluating and reporting their own progress?

Progress Tables

Level 5 Mass Production	Level 4 System Initiation	Level 3 System Development	Level 2 System Maturity	Level 1 System Excellence
• The need for appropriate control indicators (measurables) for tracking progress toward established targets is not recognized • No effective means of auditing and verifying implementation of companywide policies	• Each area establishes its own measures, but— • The control indicators selected are often abstract and do not distinguish differences in concrete objectives between levels • Reporting mechanisms exist but reporting is haphazard or on demand, and usefulness of information varies	• Concrete, consistent measures of improvement and clear target values are identified in each area and level • A regular audit process and reporting procedure is established, but not adhered to in all areas • Not all managers understand their role in the audit process • Teams collect data, but do not consistently understand its usefulness	• Visual management tools help assure that the link between policy, results, and improvement plans is clear • Vertical reporting mechanisms are effective but some misconnects still occur between functions at the same level • Reporting procedures are understood by all managers, but Teams are not consistently involved in evaluating and reporting their own progress	• Methods for monitoring policy deployment progress and day-to-day requirements are well established and standardized • Visual tools permit at-a-glance assessment of current conditions and progress • Adjustments are handled easily • Audit processes and reporting formats are streamlined and easy to use • At every level, teams monitor, evaluate and report on their own progress

Lean Management Reference Table

	Cornerstone	Strategy
Key 2	Leadership	
	Control Point	2.5 Reflection

Diagnostic Questions

- Has the company established a system to ensure that critical gaps in performance are identified and addressed in next year's strategic plan?
- Does cross-functional management support easy access to information for planning?
- Can the system capture emerging strategic ideas at all levels of the company?

Progress Tables

Level 5 Mass Production	Level 4 System Initiation	Level 3 System Development	Level 2 System Maturity	Level 1 System Excellence
• No gathering or analysis of previous year's experience, only review of results • Poor interdepartmental relationships make it difficult to clearly identify and prioritize problems	• Amount and type of data collected can be improved • Differences between targets and actual results are reviewed but not analyzed • Plans are not reviewed together, e.g., no cross-functional management	• Target/actual analysis continuous and consistent with PDCA, but • Insufficient feedback of monitored results for next year's planning cycle • Cross-functional management present but weak • Information gathered still consists mainly of results, input of strategic ideas limited	• Feedback for next planning cycle is good, e.g., progress to plans is easy to assess • Cross-functional management good but not consistent throughout company • System in place to gather strategic ideas from the lowest level to the highest	• Feedback procedures are standardized, streamlined and adhered to, easy access to companywide results, analysis and innovative ideas • Planning and management across departments is excellent and supports easy top management analysis of performance to targets companywide

Lean Management Reference Table

		Cornerstone	Structure
Key 3	Lean Organization	**Control Point**	3.1 Team Activities

Diagnostic Questions

- Does the company effectively employ small-group activities at every level and on a companywide basis to solve problems and make improvements?
- Does the company have a well-organized system for engaging work groups and improvement teams in an ongoing companywide drive to improve processes and operations?

Progress Tables

Level 5	Level 4	Level 3	Level 2	Level 1
Mass Production	**System Initiation**	**System Development**	**System Maturity**	**System Excellence**
• No desire to establish teams or workgroups, or start small-group activities • Military-style chain-of-command; "commanders" coordinate most of the activity • Employees viewed as chess pieces	• Interest in small-group activities and team-building develops; sense of community and group culture begins to emerge • Management sees need to transform and manage cultural variables to support world class methods and high technology • Pilot projects are established and an implementation schedule • Management has strategy, but team members must coordinate own moves • Employees viewed as members of a cooperative team • Participation is limited • Some competition among teams and small groups, but not linked to company policy	• Emerging culture supports cross-functional management, teams, and empowerment • Based on customer orientation, shared information, visual management, and intensive training • Teams established in most main areas, but not fully developed • Good system support for small groups in place, but links to company policy still unclear • Team activities supported with training, resources, and time for participation • Improvement corners established in major areas	• Teams in major areas are mature • Teams exist in most supporting areas • Company policy determines improvement initiatives • Small-group activities are generally active, enthusiastic, and clearly linked to company goals • Team culture is continuously refined through team members feedback to management • Team training and activities integrated with comprehensive employee education program • Teams are highly motivated (competitive)	• Small-group activities are vital and well integrated with company policy • The top management team has matured • Several teams within the company have achieved high performance • Competition system is a well-established feature of company culture

Lean Management Reference Table

	Cornerstone	Structure
Key 3	Lean Organization	**Control Point**	3.2 Networked Organization

Diagnostic Questions

- How many levels of management exist within the company?
- Is the company structured for organizational learning?
- Has the company installed a team-based organization that minimizes bureaucratic drag on decision making and action?
- Is a system of overlapping teams in place to open channels of communication vertically—from management to the shop floor—and horizontally—across functions?
- Does the organizational structure support empowerment of workgroups and individuals?

- Can individual and team goals be aligned easily with the company's overall targets?
- Has the company established appropriate committees, teams, and reporting structures to cross-functionally manage value delivery and supporting processes?
- Do cross-functional teams effectively focus expertise and resources on strategic initiatives and chronic problems?
- Is authority balanced between cross-functional team managers and functional department heads?

Progress Tables

Level 5	Level 4	Level 3	Level 2	Level 1
Mass Production	**System Initiation**	**System Development**	**System Maturity**	**System Excellence**
• No clear organization except for boss at the top • Arbitrary decision making (runs like a labor camp) • No definition of roles • Lines of authority nonexistent • Cross-functional committees initiated to solve chronic problems or help manage strategic initiatives • Misconnects and disconnects identified	• Lines of authority are clear, but no one is sure how to carry out management's objectives • Objectives are unquantified and nonspecific, e.g., "safety first" • Most managers do not participate in planning cycle • Most departments do not have a process for turning objectives into concrete action plans (who does what, when and how in appropriate detail) • Cross-functional committees in most major areas, but committee heads and team leaders are not full-time • Misconnects and disconnects reduced	• Rational organization and division of responsibilities • Clear instruction from the top with objectives broken down and quantified clearly at each level • Everyone tracks progress on goals visually • Organization reasonably effective, but dictatorial processes and excessive sign-offs may slow down decision making • Feedback from lower levels is inadequate; poor two-way communication • Need shared goals and commitment beyond simple agreement • Team activity to meet goals is not always aligned with objectives • Full-time multifunctional team leaders are also members of top management team • Misconnects and disconnects are infrequent • Department managers still hold balance of power	• Team-based organization with good vector alignment • Systems in place to assure vector alignment, e.g., interlevel coordination (interlocking teams) and regular meetings • Some individuals lack skills needed to work flexibly within work teams • Some teams lack skills and knowledge to respond quickly and easily to changes on strategic direction • Power is balanced between multifunctional team managers and department heads • Misconnects and disconnects virtually eliminated • Firm continuously reengineers itself • Zero bureaucracy	• An "all-weather" organization that can respond flexibly to changing needs • Goals, objectives are complete, appropriate and quantified • Well-established system for team and individual development • Well-established system for responding to changing needs and reframing objectives to meet those needs

Lean Management Reference Table

		Cornerstone	Structure
Key 3	Lean Organization	**Control Point**	3.3 Rewards and Recognition

Diagnostic Questions

- Has the company installed appropriate mechanisms for routinely recognizing good performance and employee and team contributions to company improvement goals?
- Are rewards tailored to reflect specific needs and preferences of the company's own employees?

Progress Tables

Level 5	Level 4	Level 3	Level 2	Level 1
Mass Production	System Initiation	System Development	System Maturity	System Excellence
• Management recognition of employees is sporadic, typically private, and often arbitrary • There is no system for recognizing and rewarding employee contributions outside of the compensation system	• Employee contributions are recognized and rewarded through suggestion schemes • Team competition is encouraged • Links between suggestion system and company improvement initiatives are weak • Management still believes employees are motivated solely by monetary rewards	• A flexible system for recognizing team and individual employee contributions is established • System is based on balanced monetary and nonmonetary motivators	• Recognition system is refined so recognition and rewards are clearly linked to company policy • Managers have carefully studied what motivates company's workforce	

Lean Management Reference Table

Key 3	Lean Organization	Cornerstone	Structure
		Control Point	3.4 Evaluation and Compensation

Diagnostic Questions

- Does the company evaluate performance in a way that supports organizational learning?
- Does the company evaluate performance in a way that encourages teamwork, personal development, and the sharing of vital information?
- Are compensation systems designed to promote teamwork by making some portion of variable pay dependent on the success of the employee's workgroup, team, or the company as a whole?

Progress Tables

Level 5	Level 4	Level 3	Level 2	Level 1
Mass Production	**System Initiation**	**System Development**	**System Maturity**	**System Excellence**
• Subjective opinions rather than companywide performance objectives goals drive evaluations • Compensation based mainly on hours and seniority	• Annual performance evaluations have some link to company goals, e.g., MBO; but— • Evaluation is still focused on individual performance • Teams are not evaluated separately • Company uses performance-based pay, but not linked to company or team goals • Performance pay is mainly for managers	• Performance evaluations match company policy and are attentive to team and individual performance, but— • Value of feedback is diluted by long delays • Some portion of pay is based on gainsharing, loosely linked to company and/or team goals • Performance pay is for all workers		• In each work area built-in (visual) performance indicators let employees evaluate their own, workgroup, and team performance daily • Management evaluations are diagnostic, not critical • Some portion of pay is based on gainsharing and is clearly linked to company and/or team goals • Employees have flexible compensation package tailored to individual needs

Lean Management Reference Table

		Cornerstone	Structure
Key 3	Lean Organization	**Control Point**	3.5 Lean Administration

Diagnostic Questions

- Has the company applied process mapping and industrial engineering concepts to reengineer its administrative and support processes?
- Have the company's office environments established a vital system of team-based improvement activities?
- Are the 5S's and visual control systems applied as rigorously in the office as on the shop floor?
- Do office workgroups strive continuously to eliminate waste by reducing the space, time, and number of steps, signatures, and interdepartmental handoffs required for routine tasks and processes?

Progress Tables

Level 5 Mass Production	Level 4 System Initiation	Level 3 System Development	Level 2 System Maturity	Level 1 System Excellence
• Administration and support services operate independently from value-delivery processes • All employees work in separate offices and cubicles, "silos" of process and information • Big gap perceived between white- and blue-collar work • Administrative processes can be time-consuming, error-prone, inflexible, redundant, wasteful • The form of information produced suits its producers better than its intended customers • Control mechanisms aim to produce adherence to procedures rather than to improve procedure results	• Pilot projects in selected areas to create information production lines by streamlining and reorganizing processes • Initiatives in all areas to eliminate unnecessary items, reorganize and control what remains (5S) • Systematic measurement and analysis of administrative losses in purchasing, subcontracting, administrative work, distribution, and inventory • Increased awareness of need to reduce administrative and support cycle times • Increased awareness in administration and support services of their supporting roles in production and equipment management	• Redesign in all major administrative and support areas using process mapping, ECRS*, and industrial engineering concepts • Innovative, people-serving uses of space • Space-saving, economical, shared information storage (public files, libraries, tools) • Workplace organization (5S) implemented in all major administrative and support areas • Administrative losses visibly reduced • Regular management audits *ECRS = Eliminate, Combine, Rearrange, Simplify	• Continuous improvement redesign of administrative and support areas centers on preparing for and installing appropriate automation • Workplace organization efforts focus on standardization and refinement of controls • 50% reduction of steps in administrative and support process	• New streamlined processes are visually controlled and easy to follow • 67% reduction of administrative and support process steps • Workplace organization efforts focus on achieving universal awareness and individual adherence

Lean Management Reference Table

		Cornerstone	Structure
Key 4	Partnering	**Control Point**	4.1 Employee Value

Diagnostic Questions

- Does the company analyze employee morale systematically and scientifically, and are the results of this analysis reflected in the company's strategic plan and policy?

- How well does the company manage its human resources? Does the company have a positive philosophy towards employees?
- Are employees and their knowledge of best practices—recognized as a critical factor in the competitive success of the enterprise?
- Has the company demonstrated a commitment to the intensive training of its workforce in best practices?
- Does the company provide each employee with paths to personal and career development that encourage personal and organizational learning?

Progress Tables

Level 5	Level 4	Level 3	Level 2	Level 1
Mass Production	**System Initiation**	**System Development**	**System Maturity**	**System Excellence**
• Employees are viewed by management as disposable labor—an expense • Employees are not expected to contribute anything to the enterprise beyond the labor demanded and directed by managers • Enterprise obligation to employees is perceived as monetary—payment for services rendered	• Employees are valued as assets • Employee skills and experience are acknowledged as valuable contributions to the enterprise • The enterprise is obliged to manage human assets properly to guarantee a good return on investment, primarily and through rewards recognition	• Employees are understood as a potential resource for adding value within the enterprise • Employee knowledge, skills, and experience are actively cultivated through training and career-planning programs • Management invests in its employees by underwriting external education and establishing pay-for-knowledge programs	• Employees are recognized as a critical factor in the success of the enterprise • Individual knowledge and creativity, in addition to skills and experience, are actively cultivated • Recognizing that employees can contribute creatively and powerfully to the bottom line, management invests in organizational changes that support a dynamic learning environment	• Employees are understood as the essential heart and value of the enterprise • Employees are expected and permitted to take full responsibility for the well-being and growth of the enterprise • Organizationally, all employees are treated as dynamic partners in the enterprise and share in the profits it generates

Lean Management Reference Table

		Cornerstone	Structure
Key 4	Partnering	Control Point	4.2 Comakership

Diagnostic Questions

- Has the company established effective procedures to manage its relationships with suppliers to ensure high quality and on-time delivery?
- Has the company established effective procedures to help suppliers improve their quality, cost, and delivery?
- Does the company provide consulting or training to suppliers to help suppliers develop better capabilities?
- Has the company established effective procedures to involve suppliers in product development?

Progress Tables

Level 5 Mass Production	Level 4 System Initiation	Level 3 System Development	Level 2 System Maturity	Level 1 System Excellence
• Unqualified suppliers are numerous • Price determines purchase inputs • All designs to suppliers are from company • Leadership and support not provided for supplier development • Supplier feedback limited to information on supplier costs • Short-term contracts and arms-length dealings define supplier relationships	• Management begins to monitor supplier performance, identifies problem suppliers • Self-certification encouraged • Supplier QCD feedback solicited on new designs before finalization • Technical support is given on request for any subcontracted component, material, or service • Long-term contracts are offered to best suppliers	• A company certification program helps reduce the number of suppliers • Certified suppliers offered long-term contracts based on quality, cost, delivery, and potential for improvement • Industrial engineering support provided on each supplier line • Suppliers more closely involved in design of new product development	• Long-term partnerships are formed with suppliers demonstrating ability to improve • The company invests in the quality of its suppliers by providing concrete quality guidance and assistance • Leadership and support provided to bring partners to world class status • Supply partners are actively involved in product development from the earliest early stages	• Long-term partnerships are strengthened • Suppliers sustaining a record of continuous improvement and high quality are treated as partners • Sustained leadership and support for supplier development • Supply partners are integral members of product development teams

Lean Management Reference Table

		Cornerstone	Structure
Key 4	Partnering	**Control Point**	4.3 Environmental Impact

Diagnostic Questions

- Has the company established effective programs that ensure environmental safety by employing appropriate technology and improving equipment effectiveness?

Progress Tables

Level 5	Level 4	Level 3	Level 2	Level 1
Mass Production	**System Initiation**	**System Development**	**System Maturity**	**System Excellence**
• Low awareness of environmental impact of products and processes • Occasional infringement of environmental regulations	• Company begins studying its impact on the environment • Initiates programs to improve environment with appropriate technology and equipment improvement activities	• Companywide programs for improving environmental conditions established • Compliance with environmental regulations is substantially improved	• Full compliance with environmental regulations in each market	• Provides leadership in environmental affairs • Useful to government as information source for solving environmental problems

Lean Management Reference Table

		Cornerstone	Structure
Key 4	Partnering	Control Point	4.4 Social Integrity

Diagnostic Questions

- Is the company a good corporate citizen?
- Has the company established programs that ensure community health and safety through better products and more useful information, or through contributions to education, art, or science?

Progress Tables

Level 5 Mass Production	Level 4 System Initiation	Level 3 System Development	Level 2 System Maturity	Level 1 System Excellence
• Little awareness of company's role in the communities where its products are manufactured and where it sells products and services • Frequent misunderstandings with local agencies	• Company examines its role within the community • Community improvement programs are initiated (e.g., improving product safety, cooperating in local education for future workers) • Some communications and public relations problems still occur	• Companywide programs for promoting employee and community welfare (e.g., health, education, culture) • Communications networks established to reduce disconnects between company and community agencies • Compliance record and public relations substantially improved	• Company perceived as an important player in community affairs • Company-community communications are regular, seamless, and productive • Full compliance with government regulations in each market achieved	• Company provides leadership in public affairs • Local government values company as a resource in solving community problems

Lean Management Reference Table

		Cornerstone	Structure
Key 5	Information Architecture	**Control Point**	5.1 Workplace Organization and Visual Control

Diagnostic Questions

- Has the company established effective procedures for industrial housekeeping and workplace organization companywide?
- Does every object have an address, and a return address label?
- Are the locations of teams, equipment, tools, and inventory and the flow of production visually clear?
- Has the company established effective companywide visual control systems to ensure that information is available at point-of-use?

Progress Tables

Level 5 Mass Production	Level 4 System Initiation	Level 3 System Development	Level 2 System Maturity	Level 1 System Excellence
• The workplace is dirty, cluttered, and disorganized • Searching for vital tools, dies, materials, documents, and personnel is time consuming • Information on standards and abnormalities is not readily available • Frequent abnormalities create confusion	• Workplace organization program initiated, unnecessary items are removed • Floors and work areas are clear, but passageways and pillars are used for temporary storage • Proper locations are not readily apparent • Cleaning and organizing initiatives are intermittent; some backsliding occurs • Managers use signs and wall charts to share information on standards, but— • Workers lack complete information and the ability to effectively prevent problems	• Workplace is clean and clear on all horizontal and vertical surfaces • Workers encouraged to create visual controls that enhance organization such as outlining, addressing, and labeling • Visitors can see clearly what goes where in main work areas, but storage areas, closed cabinets, and drawers are disorganized • Control boards and other visual systems are used to share important information immediately and build standards into the workplace • Critical abnormalities are easier to identify	• Workplace and storage areas are clean, well organized, and visually managed • Cleanliness and organization are maintained by regular audits based on detailed checklists for each area • Personnel take pride in the environment and discipline is high • Teams develop poka-yoke devices to effectively prevent critical abnormalities • Company strategy is apparent to all; abnormalities are perceived immediately	• Workplace is immaculate and "transparent"; workforce is highly disciplined • At-a-glance visual control of workflow, inventory, and all operating and work area standards • Cleaning is reduced or eliminated by solutions that control dirt and contamination at their sources • All employees continuously improve visual control systems to enhance transparency and adherence to standards • All abnormalities are immediately corrected or prevented

Lean Management Reference Table

	Cornerstone	Structure
Key 5 Information Architecture	**Control Point**	5.2 Fast Feedback Systems

Diagnostic Questions

- Has the company established effective procedures to involve employees in recognizing, reporting, and correcting errors, defects, and process or equipment abnormalities?

Progress Tables

Level 5	Level 4	Level 3	Level 2	Level 1
Mass Production	**System Initiation**	**System Development**	**System Maturity**	**System Excellence**
• No internal inspection procedures—the customer is the inspector • Quality results are sent to managers who decide how to address problems • Operators may know when defects are generated but are seldom involved in solutions	• Random-sampling inspections at end of line by trained inspectors • Defect information is compiled in reports and given to engineers to troubleshoot quality problems • Operators may be queried about the events surrounding defect generation	• Inspection by trained inspectors at end of line or various points along the way • SPC online improves overall production and achieves lower AQL defect rates • Defect information collected by centralized QC/SPC department and selectively passed to engineers for troubleshooting • Operators are expected to participate on quality project teams	• Each operator inspects own work; next operator reinspects it before beginning operation • Defect information is collected continuously and used by operators to target quality improvements in their operations • Operators are encouraged to stop operations as soon as defects are discovered; engineers and supervisors come to the site immediately to troubleshoot, correct and countermeasure	• Defect information is replaced by error information which operators and engineers use to develop poka-yoke devices and other preventive solutions

Lean Management Reference Table

		Cornerstone	Structure
Key 5	Information Architecture	**Control Point**	5.3 Performance Measurement

Diagnostic Questions

- Does the company's performance measurement system provide appropriate and timely feedback for improving value delivery and supporting processes?
- Can performance measures be linked readily to policy targets, budgets, income statements, and balance sheets?
- Does the company have a realistic understanding of product costs?
- Is overhead allocated according to causal links between resource consumption and value-adding activities?

Progress Tables

Level 5 Mass Production	Level 4 System Initiation	Level 3 System Development	Level 2 System Maturity	Level 1 System Excellence
• Results-based performance measures used exclusively without awareness that they may hinder continuous improvement • Direct labor-hours determine allocation of overhead • Firm unaware of large discrepancy between estimated and actual product/service costs	• Top management team makes "balanced scorecard" of process-based measures to provide timely feedback for corrective action and improvement • Old measurement system is still in operation • New accounting system allocates overhead according to demonstrated causal links between resource consumption and value-adding activities, but— • Company still operates on old accounting system	• New process-based scorecard deployed to managers and supervisors, runs alongside old results-based measures • Although financial measures are still more important, their inefficiency is quite apparent • New accounting system deployed to managers and supervisors, runs parallel with old system	• Performance-based measures improved • Old results-based measures are abandoned except those supporting clear cause-and-effect analysis • Improvements made to new accounting system; old system is abandoned with exception of required external reports	• New system integrated fully with performance measurement system • Modeling of financial implications of various policy alternatives during policy analysis and definition

Lean Management Reference Table

Key 5	Information Architecture	Cornerstone	Structure
		Control Point	5.4 Kaizen Reporting

Diagnostic Questions

- Does the company maintain a vital suggestion system that ensures quick evaluation of ideas and swift implementation, reward, and recognition for ideas that further company goals?
- Does the company have a well-organized system for publicizing successful methods and making sure individuals throughout the company can get the knowledge, training, and resources they need to implement those methods in their own work areas?

Progress Tables

Level 5 Mass Production	Level 4 System Initiation	Level 3 System Development	Level 2 System Maturity	Level 1 System Excellence
• Suggestion systems are mere formalities • Visual management is not used to monitor progress toward goals • Improvement activities are ad hoc and undocumented • Effective improvements are not laterally deployed to other areas	• Firm plans and sets up a suggestion system • Information on some management measures is occasionally reported in the form of graphs or charts, but is only available to selected managers • The results of improvement activities are reported to managers, but rarely documented or shared with other teams • Lateral deployment of improvements occurs on an ad hoc basis, when individuals become aware of improvements in other areas	• Suggestion system works, but feedback on employees slow and rate is fewer than 1 suggestion per employee per month • Suggestions not well linked to company strategy and rewards are inappropriate • Results are reported visually on a regular basis to management teams but not trended • Improvement results are reported widely to teams, but rarely documented • Lateral deployment is acknowledged as an important strategy by teams, members begin to search for ways to facilitate it	• Weekly or biweekly feedback and rewards include cash and recognition • Suggestions are linked to company policy and increase to 2 suggestions per employee per month • Results are reported regularly and trended to everyone, but are not broken down in sufficient detail to reflect shopfloor improvement activities • Improvement results and ideas are reported widely and also documented in writing • Lateral deployment is actively encouraged by management; key projects and results earmarked for deployment and shared with relevant teams	• Employees focus on implemented ideas and take responsibility for coordinating and testing • Rewards include gainsharing and improve to 5 or more suggestions per employee per month • Visual reporting is universal and motivating; tied to management objectives and clearly broken down at every level • Improvement results and ideas are documented in a form easy to access and transfer and are standardized companywide • The potential for and scope of lateral deployment are considered at the outset of every project and a standard procedure is established to assure that ideas are effectively deployed

Lean Management Reference Table

		Cornerstone	Strengths
Key 6	Culture of Improvement	**Control Point**	6.1 Standardization

Diagnostic Questions

- Have all procedures for all operations in all departments of the company been studied and effectively standardized to ensure adherence and support continuous improvement?
- Are employees involved in setting standards for their own work?
- Are standards made clear through visual controls, including poka-yoke (mistake-proofing) devices?
- Can standards be updated easily?

Progress Tables

Level 5 Mass Production	Level 4 System Initiation	Level 3 System Development	Level 2 System Maturity	Level 1 System Excellence
• Operating procedures generally left to each individual's discretion • No way to tell if job is done the same way twice • Shopfloor data thoroughly unreliable • Statistics are useless, sometimes misleading	• Operating procedures vaguely standardized in roughly the same order • Standards set for major processes but, for lack of visual controls, are ineffective • Rough benchmarks can be set • Data quality improving	• All processes, most operations have standard procedures, but are still unclear to office and online workers • System for updating standards is sound but implementation is ineffective • Data more reliable	• Standards visually clear • Changes in standards communicated in timely effective way • Standards updated based on input from workers, especially managers and engineers • Data is trusted	• Standards continuously updated based on workers' innovations and input from managers and engineering • Data is reliable and directly supports continuous improvement

Lean Management Reference Table

		Cornerstone	Strengths
Key 6	Culture of Improvement		6.2 Waste-Free Strategy
		Control Point	

Diagnostic Questions

- Does the company have an effective program for identifying and eliminating all forms of non-value-adding waste in all operations, including inventory and delays?
- Does every employee understand and apply the concept of "value-adding"?

Progress Tables

Level 5	Level 4	Level 3	Level 2	Level 1
Mass Production	**System Initiation**	**System Development**	**System Maturity**	**System Excellence**
• Value-adding and non-value-adding operations are not differentiated • Improvement is unsystematic, typically responding to bottleneck of the moment	• People have a common understanding about the nature of waste and begin categorizing value-adding and non-value-adding activities in every process • Improvement focuses on eliminating non-value-adding wastes (e.g., transportation, unnecessary motion or searching, overproduction, inventory, defects and scrap, equipment-related wastes, inspection, information, and creativity)	• Teams in all areas make concrete plans and pursue activities to increase overall value-adding rate by reducing critical wastes (value-adding time divided by total time less planned breaks and planned downtime)	• Improvement activities have raised overall value-adding rate to 85% or better • All analysis, planning, and continuous improvement activities are driven by the zero-waste principle • Teams adopt a companywide effort to further reduce waste; all improvement activities are coordinated to maximize waste reduction in the company	• Improvement activities have raised the rate to 95% or better

Lean Management Reference Table

	Cornerstone	Strengths
Key 6	Culture of Improvement	
	Control Point	6.3 Technology Diffusion

Diagnostic Questions

- Does the company culture support organizational learning and continuous improvement of products and processes?
- Do the company's managers and engineers understand that technology is embedded in production methods, i.e., step-by-step procedures, as well as in equipment?
- How quickly can the organization as a whole diffuse a new technology (transfer new learning to other units)?
- Does the company diffuse new methods through high-speed training and other means across the organization?

Progress Tables

Level 5 Mass Production	Level 4 System Initiation	Level 3 System Development	Level 2 System Maturity	Level 1 System Excellence
• No interest in other players in the industry • Content with status • Technology transfer occurs because engineers tell people what to do • Some ideas disseminated by word of mouth • Knowledge and practice of workers not considered part of site technology • No interest in Value Analysis	• Company sees itself as one step behind the industry • Lacks ability to assimilate new technology • Managers understand new methods • Method transfer is done through general teaching materials and examples of improvements in model lines and information boards • Systematic improvement of each process is beginning • Transfer is still sporadic • Poor retention of new methods	• Factory on a par with industry • Special training conducted with high-level texts and videos • Transfer is more systematic • Understanding and retention of new methods is improving • Improvements are made in every process	• Company one step ahead of industry average • Able to assimilate new technology • High-speed training is based on adult learning techniques • Training on workers' own equipment is established • One-point lessons are used on the job • Retention is good • Improvements are made on factory-scale processes • Each section reduces steps by 50%	• Site technology leads the industry • Basic technology and new technology are on the leading edge • Refined system established for continuous training and retraining of office staff and machine operators in best practices • All improvements are done systematically • Steps reduces by two-thirds • FMS being considered

Lean Management Reference Table

		Cornerstone	Strengths
Key 6	Culture of Improvement		
		Control Point	6.4 Education

Diagnostic Questions

- How well does the company educate and train its personnel?
- Has the company established an effective system for training personnel intensively and continuously in world class methods on their own equipment?
- Are supervisors involved in the delivery of training?
- Where appropriate, do employees receive specialized education to close strategic gaps in performance or to improve morale?
- Is the company capable of providing specialized education and training as necessary?

Progress Tables

Level 5 Mass Production	Level 4 System Initiation	Level 3 System Development	Level 2 System Maturity	Level 1 System Excellence
• Only managers and new employees receive training • Technology transfer only occurs when engineers tell people what to do • Some ideas disseminated by word of mouth • Knowledge and practice of workers not considered part of site technology; skill versatility is not valued	• General recognition that methods are technology and skill versatility is valuable • OJT carried out informally by workers themselves— primarily "one-on-one" • Skill improvement initiatives begin within groups • Employees trained to recognize abnormalities and opportunities for improvement, use statistics and cause-and-effect logic • Methods are transferred informally through individual study, team exposure to improvements done in other areas, and reports posted on information boards • Transfer remains sporadic • Retention of new methods is poor • Most training funds still spent on managers	• Training funds are allocated to train the total workforce • Cross-training occurs within work groups • OJT for new employees is standardized and delivered by work team members • One-point lessons are used for cross-training and continuous work team OJT • Employees are trained to communicate effectively with managers, supervisors, and peers • New skill or skill improvement training is conducted with purchased texts and videos • Transfer is more systematic • Understanding and retention of new methods improves	• Training becomes a major initiative; e.g., equivalent of 10% of payroll is spent on training • Cross-training occurs between job groups • New skill or skill improvement training is done systematically by marshaling in-house expertise to design customized training material, and by using external certificate programs and outside trainers and consultants • One-point lessons are collected in operating manuals and are continually upgraded to facilitate transfer • Training in problem recognition, problem solving, communication skills reinforced and extended • Training materials and formats emphasize adult learning techniques and practical application with trainees own equipment • Retention is good • All employees know their role with information—how to interpret, when to share, how to build in to production and support processes	• Employees themselves carry out R&D of new methods and technology • Continuous training and retraining of office staff and machine operators in best practices is systematized • Company is a cybernetic network of highly aware, logical, communicative employees • Organizational learning is continuous • Innovation occurs every day

Lean Management Reference Table

	Cornerstone	Strengths
Key 7	Lean Production	
	Control Point	7.1 Flow Production

Diagnostic Questions

- Does the layout of the company's factories apply advanced industrial engineering concepts effectively to increase efficiency and flexibility by reducing lot sizes, inventory, and staffing requirements?

Progress Tables

Level 5 Mass Production	Level 4 System Initiation	Level 3 System Development	Level 2 System Maturity	Level 1 System Excellence
• Job shop layout; large lots accumulate near machines and operators, each process moves at own pitch (rhythm)	• Job shop layout; some small lot production and reliance on conveyance systems • Successful pilot JIT cell formed	• Cellular and in-line layouts are geared for single process, small lot flow	• Cellular and in-line layouts are geared for one-piece flow within and between processes	• Full multiprocess operations with one-piece flow

Lean Management Reference Table

		Cornerstone	Strengths
Key 7	Lean Production	Control Point	7.2 Multiprocess Handling

Diagnostic Questions

- Is the company's workforce flexible in skills and knowledge?
- Do employees understand the company's equipment and processes well enough to respond to bottlenecks and handle unpredictable swings in market demand?

Progress Tables

Level 5 Mass Production	Level 4 System Initiation	Level 3 System Development	Level 2 System Maturity	Level 1 System Excellence
• Unquestioned support for single-skill, single-process operations	• Single-skill, single process operations with some cooperation among operators at adjacent processes	• Flow-based, cooperative operations • Workers capable of helping next worker "upstream" and "downstream"	• Flow-based cooperative operations • Workers can handle about half the processes in a cell, are capable of helping in other cells and on other lines • Flexible job assignments with wide variation between workers in quality and volume of output	• Operators can handle all processes in a cell • Flexible job assignments, with little variation in quality and volume of output

Lean Management Reference Table

		Cornerstone	Strengths
Key 7	Lean Production	Control Point	7.3 Leveled, Mixed Model Production

Diagnostic Questions

- Does the company practice just-in-time internally?
- Is the schedule flexible enough to respond to the marketplace?

Progress Tables

Level 5	Level 4	Level 3	Level 2	Level 1
Mass Production	System Initiation	System Development	System Maturity	System Excellence
• Production as it comes • Monthly production schedule; processes have own rhythms	• Fixed lots • Biweekly production schedule; each process has its own rhythm • Opportunities identified for cellular manufacturing and mixed model production • Product families are identified	• Application of group technology (processing similar parts together) for major product families • Weekly production schedule, overall line is roughly synchronized	• Integrated processing cycle • Mixed model production begins • Daily production runs; in-line production with specific cycle times	• Mixed model processing • Completely level production, plantwide synchronization • Capable of mixed-model production

Lean Management Reference Table

	Cornerstone	Strengths
Key 7	Lean Production	**Control Point**	7.4 Quick Changeover

Diagnostic Questions

- Has the company studied the costs associated with downtime resulting from changeover?
- Are all changeovers routinely performed in under ten minutes?
- Where necessary, is the company equipped to perform changeovers in under three minutes (or within one machine cycle)?

Progress Tables

Level 5 Mass Production	Level 4 System Initiation	Level 3 System Development	Level 2 System Maturity	Level 1 System Excellence
• 1 or 2 changeovers per month, regardless of customer requirements, taking as much as half a day each	• Management studies impact of changeovers on plant capacity and flexibility • People aware of changeover needs • Die change analysis and pilot changeover improvement projects begun	• Changeover teams active in most major areas • All employees trained in quick changeover techniques • Changeover times decreasing	• "One-touch exchange of die" implemented on bottleneck equipment • Ten-minute maximum on all changeovers	• Changeovers done within cycle times • Changeovers automated where necessary • FMS used where necessary to ensure precise control

Lean Management Reference Table

Key 7	Cornerstone	Strengths
Lean Production	Control Point	7.5 Automation with a Human Touch

Diagnostic Questions

- Has the company automated unpleasant and unsafe tasks?
- Is the company's equipment capable of unmonitored, defect-free production?
- Are line workers involved in developing poka-yoke (mistake-proofing) devices to ensure adherence to standards?

Progress Tables

Level 5	Level 4	Level 3	Level 2	Level 1
Mass Production	System Initiation	System Development	System Maturity	System Excellence
• All processes require manual assistance • No understanding that equipment monitoring is wasteful	• Some automation exists, but operators always present while machines work • Wastefulness of monitoring thoroughly understood • Some equipment can run one unmonitored cycle during lunch	• Human and machine work are separated • Major equipment can run one unmonitored cycle during lunch, but— • Machines still sometimes make defects	• Human and machine work are separated • Most machines run unmonitored during lunch; many machines left cycling after operators depart • Machines still sometimes make defects, but poka-yoke applied actively	• Human and machine work are separated • Machines make no defects • Firm is capable of FMS

Lean Management Reference Table

	Cornerstone	Strengths
Key 7	Lean Production	
	Control Point	7.6 Pull System/ Coupled Production

Diagnostic Questions

- Does the company effectively use kanban cards, designated floor squares, bins, or other "pull" signals to minimize handling and inventory and to link production more closely to market demand?
- Are kanban methods deployed to suppliers as well?

Progress Tables

Level 5	Level 4	Level 3	Level 2	Level 1
Mass Production	**System Initiation**	**System Development**	**· System Maturity**	**System Excellence**
• Push production • Inventory is retained • Inventory stored everywhere	• Push production, with organized storage sites for WIP • All employees understand importance of coupling points between processes • Coupling points are established between major processes	• Coupling points established throughout factory • Pull production, with fixed locations and fixed volumes • Kanban implementation begins in pilot areas	• Pull production, with kanban • Individual cells combine into lines	• Pull production, with refined kanban • Short lines are organized into long lines • Many coupling points eliminated

Lean Management Reference Table

		Cornerstone	Strengths
Key 7	Lean Production	**Control Point**	7.7 Production Scheduling

Diagnostic Questions

- Does the company schedule production daily according to market demand as well as its business plan?
- Do production lines, including major processes and subprocesses, have a common rhythm?
- Have both late deliveries and overproduction been eliminated?

Progress Tables

Level 5	Level 4	Level 3	Level 2	Level 1
Mass Production	**System Initiation**	**System Development**	**System Maturity**	**System Excellence**
• Production manually scheduled once a month • No relation between production schedule, business plan, and strategy • Processes have own rhythm • Deliveries are routinely late	• Production scheduled manually twice a month • Standard schedule control system used, but link to business plan, and strategy rather weak • Processes have own rhythm • Deliveries occasionally late	• Production scheduled weekly with computer • Some relation to business plan and strategy • Each overall line has common rhythm • Arrangements made to placate customers when deliveries are late	• Production scheduled daily and integrated with CAD when necessary • Production has clear relationship to business plan and strategy • Overall lines have a common rhythm • All deliveries are prompt • MRP and DRP used as needed	• Production scheduled daily and is completely level • Relation to business plan and strategy is strong • Overall line has common rhythm • No late deliveries

Lean Management Reference Table

	Cornerstone	Strengths
Key 8	Lean Equipment Management	
	Control Point	8.1 Equipment/ Process Improvement

Diagnostic Questions

- Does the company manage its equipment to minimize equipment-related losses and extend equipment life?
- Is the company actively improving its product quality and equipment availability and efficiency by involving maintenance personnel and engineers together on equipment improvement teams?
- Do equipment improvement teams have a well-designed program of improvement linked to the company's overall strategy and policy?
- Are equipment operators involved on teams to investigate facts and share improvement ideas with engineers and maintenance personnel?

Progress Tables

Level 5 Mass Production	Level 4 System Initiation	Level 3 System Development	Level 2 System Maturity	Level 1 System Excellence
• No ongoing improvement activities; occasional projects initiated by engineering when critical equipment fails • Some tracking of quality, uptime and equipment utilization, but equipment-related losses (OEE) are not measured as such • Ineffective communication between production, engineering, and maintenance	• Equipment loss is baselined and monitored in critical areas and on critical machines • Cross-functional improvement teams formed to eliminate the 8 big equipment losses, especially on equipment that constrains production • Critical equipment selected for analysis and overhaul (model machines) • Teams coordinate improvement efforts with autonomous maintenance teams and maintenance personnel • Focus on reducing variability in failure intervals by reducing and preventing deterioration • OEE 40%—> 65%	• Model machines established in all areas • Model lines established in some critical areas (all equipment restored and improved) • Once sporadic failures are eliminated, teams focus on chronic or hidden losses • Focus on extending equipment life by addressing design weaknesses • OEE 65%—>75%	• All critical equipment and all lines are managed through TPM • Cross-functional teams establish and maintain conditions for zero defects in critical processes through quality maintenance techniques • Processes highly capable, but variability still too high • OEE 75%—>85%	• Many lines reporting zero defects regularly • Variability very low • OEE at least 85% or better

Lean Management Reference Table

		Cornerstone	Strengths
Key 8	Lean Equipment Management	**Control Point**	8.2 Autonomous Maintenance

Diagnostic Questions

- Does the company maintain optimal equipment conditions by involving machine operators in daily inspection, cleaning, and lubrication of their own machines?
- Are operators learning equipment function and structure, e.g., mechanics, hydraulics, pneumatics, electrical systems, drive systems, etc.?
- Can operators apply this knowledge in conducting daily inspections of their own equipment, in lubricating equipment regularly, and in making occasional basic repairs, replacements, and improvements?

Progress Tables

Level 5 Mass Production	Level 4 System Initiation	Level 3 System Development	Level 2 System Maturity	Level 1 System Excellence

• High functional walls, adversarial relations, and ineffective communication among engineering, maintenance and production personnel
• If any preventive maintenance is carried out, it is performed by maintenance personnel.
• Operators "operate" equipment. When it goes down, they expect maintenance to "fix" it. Maintenance has learned not to expect cooperation from production.
	• Operator teams are formed to work with maintenance and take responsibility for establishing and maintaining optimal equipment conditions
	• Operators expose and correct equipment abnormalities
	• Steps 1, 2, and 3 of Autonomous Maintenance implemented in pilot areas:
	  1. Initial cleaning
	  2. Identify and eliminate sources of dirt and contamination
	  3. Operators create initial standards for cleaning, inspection, and lubrication
		• Working closely with maintenance engineering personnel, operators learn and understand equipment functions and structure
		• Steps 1, 2, and 3 implemented area- and companywide
		• Step 4 of Autonomous Maintenance implemented in pilot areas:
		  4. Operators are trained to conduct general equipment inspections
			• Operators learn the relation between equipment conditions and quality
			• Step 4 implemented area and companywide
			• Steps 5 and 6 of Autonomous Maintenance implemented in pilot areas:
			  5. Operators conduct general inspections autonomously
			  6. Operators organize and manage equipment and the workplace with the 5S's and visual controls
				• Autonomous Maintenance fully implemented in all areas (step 7)
				• Operator teams incorporate quality maintenance standards into their daily routines
				• Operators participate in ongoing equipment improvement activities with support of engineering and maintenance personnel

Lean Management Reference Table

		Cornerstone	Strengths
Key 8	Lean Equipment Management	**Control Point**	8.3 Planned Maintenance

Diagnostic Questions

- Does the company effectively plan and manage the regular monitoring and servicing of equipment to predict and prevent equipment-related losses?
- Are complete equipment histories maintained?
- Are predictive maintenance and condition-based monitoring methods employed?
- Are maintenance professionals involved in proactive improvement of equipment performance and maintenance efficiency?

Progress Tables

Level 5	Level 4	Level 3	Level 2	Level 1
Mass Production	System Initiation	System Development	System Maturity	System Excellence
• Most equipment is in a deteriorated condition and is repaired as it breaks down • Preventive maintenance work is seldom scheduled, often delayed, or ignored • Maintenance is planned and scheduled by hand or via a computerized system that issues work orders • Scheduled and unscheduled work proceeds with noticeable delays, frequent stockouts, inconsistent work methods and tools • Equipment manuals and related files are missing or hard to access • Individual equipment histories, where they exist, give inadequate information for failure analysis • Maintenance efficiency and performance are not measured consistently	• Maintenance department initiates use of a computerized maintenance management system to track and manage preventive and proactive maintenance activities • Specialized maintenance personnel support and coordinate restoration and PM activities with autonomous maintenance teams • Maintenance engineers and skilled trades people participate on equipment improvement teams • Critical equipment is scheduled for preventive maintenance • Equipment standards and manuals are organized, but— • Equipment histories still incomplete	• CMMS well established • Individual equipment histories are compiled • Full and comprehensible data on equipment improvements and modifications is recorded regularly for use in specifying new equipment • All major equipment is included in the PM program • All critical equipment is restored in response to equipment improvement and autonomous maintenance activities	• Condition monitoring and predictive maintenance are begun • Routine inspections and PM schedules are established for all major equipment and tasks are allocated and scheduled between maintenance and production teams • Maintenance engineering staff are involved in the design stages for new equipment development or purchase • Quality failure analyses by maintenance personnel support quality maintenance (zero defects) activities	• Maintenance personnel and engineers regularly involved in R&D • Predictive technologies are used extensively to support quality maintenance activities • Maintenance teams work continuously to upgrade skills, streamline and standardize maintenance activities, and reduce maintenance costs

Lean Management Reference Table

	Cornerstone	Strengths
Key 8	Lean Equipment Management	8.4 Quality Maintenance
	Control Point	

Diagnostic Questions

- Does the company systematically measure, analyze, and control optimal conditions of tools, dies, jigs, fixtures, and calibration equipment?
- Do operators and maintenance teams understand the relationship between equipment conditions and quality performance?
- Is 100 percent quality maintained through equipment conditions control, e.g., poka-yoke devices, visual controls, and condition monitoring?

Progress Tables

Level 5	Level 4	Level 3	Level 2	Level 1
Mass Production	**System Initiation**	**System Development**	**System Maturity**	**System Excellence**
• Quality activities only manage results, corrective action often delayed; quality performance and equipment performance are monitored separately, hiding key factors • Tools, dies, jigs, calibration equipment are in disarray and difficult to find	• Efforts to address causes of accelerated deterioration begin to reveal the connections between equipment conditions and quality performance	• Establishment of optimal equipment conditions in critical equipment reduces the array of factors influencing quality performance	• Quality is assured by identifying and controlling equipment conditions that control quality results • Zero defect conditions for equipment tools, dies, jigs, tools, and calibration equipment are studied and standardized, and managed through visual controls	• 100% quality routinely guaranteed through conditions control, using poka-yoke devices (error-prevention systems), visual controls, and condition monitoring

Lean Management Reference Table

		Cornerstone	Strengths
Key 8	Lean Equipment Management	Control Point	8.5 Early Equipment Management

Diagnostic Questions

- Are efforts made to systematically understand the causes of startup problems in new equipment?
- Do development and procurement teams work with maintenance and production engineering personnel to anticipate and prevent costly retrofitting or debugging after installation?
- Do standard procedures exist for capturing and applying the knowledge gained in startup improvement activities to prevent problems in the future?

Progress Tables

Level 5 Mass Production	Level 4 System Initiation	Level 3 System Development	Level 2 System Maturity	Level 1 System Excellence
• Installation and startup phases for new equipment and processes are lengthy and often involve extensive debugging and retrofitting • New processes often stabilize slowly, due to equipment-based quality problems and lack of fine-tuning between different parts of process, e.g., material feeding, and transfer • There is poor coordination among maintenance, production, and engineering divisions to respond to early equipment problems • There are no standard procedures for capturing and applying the knowledge gained through startup activities to prevent problems in the future	• Selected equipment improvement teams focus their efforts on resolving startup problems in newly installed equipment • Teams begin documenting types of problems occurring during startup and their solutions, but standard procedures for data capture are lacking	• Startup problems and their solutions are routinely documented in standard formats for use in subsequent equipment design/development projects • Development and procurement teams begin analyzing their processes and standards 1) to identify disconnect and misconnect points in the design/procurement process that result in startup problems, and 2) to consider how to incorporate data on startup experiences as early as possible to improve design and design processes • Efforts to prevent startup problems are coordinated with the development of MP design, LCC design and design for quality standards	• Development and procurement teams establish and test an early management system for new equipment design and procurement • Opportunities are provided for all engineering personnel to learn about and work within the new system	• Based on testing and evaluation, the early management system is improved and standardized and implemented in all areas • New equipment and product installations achieve "vertical startup" • System debugging and further streamlining continuously improve the system

Lean Management Reference Table

		Cornerstone	Strengths
Key 8	Lean Equipment Management	Control Point	8.6 Safety

Diagnostic Questions

- Has the company established effective systems for improving workplace safety?
- Does the company consider safety to be at least as important as quality?
- Are employees involved in improvement projects focused on safety?

Progress Tables

Level 5	Level 4	Level 3	Level 2	Level 1
Mass Production	System Initiation	System Development	System Maturity	System Excellence

• Firm conducts only very basic safety training, if any
• Numerous accidents each year; some serious
	• Workers trained to discover, improve, eliminate unsafe operations in daily work
	• Basic safety and environment requirements are established as part of Autonomous Maintenance steps 1 and 2
	  1. Detect and correct safety problems as part of initial cleaning activities
	  2. Identify and eliminate sources of spills, leaks, dust, etc.
	• Occasional accidents each year; some serious
		• Safety procedures are incorporated in provisional cleaning, lubrication and inspection standards (Autonomous Maintenance step 3)
		• Visual controls are used to make safety abnormalities apparent and clarify corrective action
		• Equipment training as part of Autonomous Maintenance step 4 deepens everyone's understanding of equipment and processes and related safety issues
		• No major accidents
			• Employees learn about and develop safety-related poka-yoke devices (error-prevention systems)
			• Efforts to reduce failures and minor stoppages reduce opportunities for accidents
			• Damage-limitation systems are established
			• Regular, standardized safety audits by teams and management reinforce safety standards
			• No lost-time accidents
				• Everyone understands and autonomously carries out their role in safety and environment management
				• Zero accidents

Lean Management Reference Table

		Cornerstone	Strengths
Key 8	Lean Equipment Management	**Control Point**	8.7 Equipment Investment and Maintenance Prevention Design

Diagnostic Questions

- Does the company consider life cycle cost as a principal financial criterion for equipment investment?
- Does the company involve maintenance personnel and manufacturing engineers on design teams to create equipment that is maintenance free? Are operators also involved?
- Are systems in place to capture information on improvements to existing equipment and feed it back to new equipment designers?

Progress Tables

Level 5 Mass Production	Level 4 System Initiation	Level 3 System Development	Level 2 System Maturity	Level 1 System Excellence
• Finance department makes equipment investment decisions based on price and machine capacity • Maintenance and manufacturing engineering have limited or no input in purchase decisions • Life costs of current equipment are high in terms of reliability, maintainability, flexibility, operability • Shopfloor observations and improvements are not sought by or communicated to engineering and design divisions for incorporation in new equipment and processes	• Life cycle cost is considered as an investment criteria and considered in procurement and in-house design efforts • Information about reliability and maintainability improvements (R&M) on existing equipment is requested of maintenance and engineering staff and occasionally considered in planning and procurement decisions	• Design to life cycle cost and design for quality assurance are major equipment investment criteria • Information on TPM and R&M improvement activities is routinely collected by maintenance and production staff and fed back to equipment planning and procurement personnel via MP information system and maintenance failure analysis records • Equipment planning incorporates new specifications based on TPM improvements in new equipment designs	• Design for life cycle profit (flexibility) is included in equipment investment criteria • Maintenance and operating personnel and manufacturing engineers are involved in equipment planning and procurement activities from the earliest stages • Engineering and design personnel establish TPM and MP design standards for reliability, maintainability, operability, flexibility, ease of quality assurance, and safety • Maintenance and production staff regularly report failure analysis and improvement data to engineering/design division	• TPM and MP data systems are streamlined to facilitate progressive input from all divisions (production, maintenance, quality, engineering, design, etc.) • Data systems provide information that is clear and easy to incorporate in new standards and designs • All new and existing critical equipment reflects TPM and MP design principles • Maintenance and production staff meet regularly with engineering/design staff to discuss results and future requirements; information transfer is standardized

Lean Management Reference Table

		Cornerstone	Strengths
Key 9	Lean Engineering	**Control Point**	9.1 Design Process

Diagnostic Questions

- How quickly can the company bring quality products to market?
- Does the company routinely use co-located cross-functional teams to design and commission new products and equipment?
- Has the company employed team-based activities and lean administration methods (see 3.5) to eliminate waste in design processes?
- Are customers and suppliers involved in the design process?

Progress Tables

Level 5 Mass Production	Level 4 System Initiation	Level 3 System Development	Level 2 System Maturity	Level 1 System Excellence
• Design or engineering departments (marked by heavy bureaucracy) are responsible for design • Engineers and specialists sequentially working through design process steps are most responsible for design • Practice of sequential, "over-the-wall" product/equipment design • Time to market is much longer than industry average	• The design department has major responsibility for new product development, but solicits input from other departments in early development stages • Formation of first experimental cross-functional development team	• Multifunctional teams routinely used for product development • Manager of design department still controls the process	• Multifunctional teams routinely used for product development • Teams co-located physically or "virtually" through networked computers, but— • Manager of design department still controls them	• Team managers are "heavyweights" who report directly to chief executive • Team includes suppliers and customers

Lean Management Reference Table

	Cornerstone	Strengths
Key 9	Lean Engineering	
	Control Point	9.2 Product Design for Quality, Cost, and Delivery

Diagnostic Questions

- Does the company ensure high quality, low costs, and performance in the field by performing FMEA and functional deployment for quality, cost, reliability, and new technology?
- Is the production process made robust with respect to operations and materials by the application of Taguchi design of experiments?
- Is the company listening to the voice of the customer in designing the new product?

Progress Tables

Level 5 Mass Production	Level 4 System Initiation	Level 3 System Development	Level 2 System Maturity	Level 1 System Excellence
• Firm does not hear the voice of the customer • Lack of focus and coordination among functions limits firm's ability to produce products at the highest quality and cost, and in the shortest time	• Quality and cost design improvement is initiated QFD, FMEA, DFMA, DOE, Taguchi DOE, VE, DR for a pilot project (one team, one product) • Company begins to tune in to the voice of the customer • Time to market still longer than average	• Concurrent engineering teams and methods (QFD, FMEA, DFMA, DOE, Taguchi DOE, VE, DR) applied to all products • The firm extends concurrent engineering to cost engineering, reliability engineering, and technology deployment • Product planning committee introduced to identify key design problems and their solutions • The firm manages the selection of components, materials, and processes cross-functionally to simplify the production process and make it flexible • Company hears the voice of the customer • Time to market on par with industry	• CAD/CAM and computer simulation introduced (process waste has been eliminated by this phase) • Voice of the customer well integrated into new designs • Time to market shorter than average	• Demonstrates sustained industry leadership; is first to market innovative quality products • Voice of customer fully integrated into new product designs • Time to market leads the industry

Concordances to Major Productivity and Quality Awards

THIS APPENDIX SHOWS CORRELATIONS between the keys and control points of the Lean Management System and the criteria of four of the world's leading quality and productivity awards:

- Malcolm Baldrige National Quality Award (1995 criteria)
- Shingo Prize for Excellence in Manufacturing (1995–96 criteria)
- Deming Application Prize (1992 criteria for overseas companies)
- PM Excellence Prize (1995 criteria for overseas companies)

Also included are links to sections of two popular frameworks for lean management implementation: Hiroyuki Hirano's *JIT Implementation Manual,* and Iwao Kobayashi's *20 Keys to Workplace Improvement.* These cross-references will be useful to companies already using the various criteria or frameworks in prize competition or as a structure for companywide continuous improvement.

MALCOLM BALDRIGE NATIONAL QUALITY AWARD

The Malcolm Baldrige National Quality Award was created in 1987 and the first awards were given in 1988. The award was created by the United States Government, out of concern that American companies were not sufficiently knowledgeable about or practiced in world class quality methods.

The Baldrige Award is designed as a framework for companies to use in monitoring their quality systems. The criteria are updated every year and make interesting reading. The award has always emphasized customer satisfaction and financial results. Recently, the scope of the Baldrige criteria has been widened to include some factors relating to productivity. Overall, however, the award is still focused strongly on quality, and treatment of other areas is often cursory. The award criteria, however, contain informative discussions of human resource management.

The Baldrige Award scoring system is complex with weights for each criterion that may change from year to year. The award is managed by the National Institute of Standards and Technology and administered by the American Society for Quality Control.

SHINGO PRIZE FOR EXCELLENCE IN MANUFACTURING

In recognition of the work of industrial engineer and consultant Dr. Shigeo Shingo, the Shingo Prize strikes an important balance by making productivity a central focus of the prize criteria. Quality-based programs such as TQM can lead to increased bureaucracy as the company grapples with control items, checkpoints, and verification structures, but never seems to get down to the business of making things. Many national awards, including the Deming Prize and the Baldrige Award, emphasize quality, statistics, and customer satisfaction but fail to specify concrete activities that contribute to higher productivity. The Shingo Prize remedies this situation by clarifying the shopfloor practices that, when combined with good quality management, create a firm that is a strong competitor.

The Shingo Prize has an organizational partnership with the National Association of Manufacturers, and is administered by the College of Business at Utah State University.

DEMING APPLICATION PRIZE

The Deming Prize was established in 1951 by JUSE (the Union of Japanese Scientists and Engineers) to commemorate the contribution of Dr. W. Edwards Deming, an American statistician, in introduction of statistical quality control to Japanese industry. The award was begun to promote and disseminate statistical quality control methods in Japanese industry. Companies from other nations are now eligible; in 1989 Florida Power & Light became the first U.S. company to win the prize.

The Deming Prize is composed basically of two awards: the Deming Prize, which awards individuals, and the Deming Application Prize, which awards the company with outstanding performance in practicing statistical quality control approaches. The Deming Application Prize for Small Companies was set up in 1957.

Following the development of Japanese-style quality control since 1960, the subject of evaluation has become broader and more sophisticated, as can be seen by the emergence of the term "companywide quality control." To accommodate this trend, Deming Application Prize for Divisions was set up in 1965, followed by Quality Control Award for Factories in 1972.

These awards are managed by the Deming Prize Committee. JUSE serves as the secretariat and provides financial aid.

PM EXCELLENCE PRIZE

The PM Excellence Prize was established in 1964 by the Japan Institute of Plant Maintenance (JIPM) to encourage Japanese industry to increase productivity through high-grade maintenance. Since the dissemination of Total Productive Maintenance (TPM), beginning in 1971, every company examined by the JIPM for the prize has practiced TPM. Hundreds of Japanese firms are implementing TPM and applying for the PM Prize, which is now almost as prestigious as the Deming Prize in Japan and abroad. Many companies outside Japan now practice TPM and an increasing number are applying for and winning the prize.

Examination for the prize takes place in two stages. First, there is a preliminary examination to determine if the company is ready to make a full application for the prize. The full examination consists of a paper audit and an on-site audit. The paper audit records the background of the company's TPM activities, the details of its activities up to the PM examination, and the results obtained. Once the company passes the paper audit, the on-site audit takes place.

FOR FURTHER INFORMATION

Baldrige Award

American Society for Quality Control
P.O. Box 3005
Milwaukee, Wisconsin, U.S.A. 53201-3005
telephone 800-248-1946; fax 414-272-1734

Shingo Prize

The Shingo Prize for Excellence in Manufacturing
College of Business, Utah State University
Logan, Utah, U.S.A. 84322-3521
telephone 801-797-2279; fax 801 797-3440

Deming Application Prize

Union of Japanese Scientists and Engineers (JUSE)
5-10-11 Sendagaya
Shibuya-ku
Tokyo 151 Japan
telephone 03-5379-1227; fax 03-3225-1813

PM Excellence Prize

Japan Institute of Plant Maintenance
Shuwa Shiba-koen 3 chome Bldg. 5F
3-1-38 Shiba-koen, Minato-ku
Tokyo 105, Japan
telephone 03-3433-0351; fax 03-3433-8665

Notes:
- Concordances of either a comprehensive or general nature are entered with reference to Lean Management System Keys.
- Concordances of a specific nature are entered with reference to Lean Management System Control Points.
- Some criteria titles have been abbreviated for ease of reference.

Lean Management System	Lean Production Implementation Systems		Criteria of Major Quality and Productivity Awards				
Keys and Control Points	Hirano: JIT Implementation	Kobayashi: 20 Keys	Baldrige Award (ASQC)	Shingo Prize (NAM)	Deming Prize (JUSE)	PM Prize (JIPM)
1. Customer Focus			7.0 Customer Focus and Satisfaction	IV. Measured Customer Satisfaction		
1.1 Customer Requirements			7.4 Customer Satisfaction Results			
1.2 Customer Relationships			7.2 Customer Relationship Management			
1.3 Order-to-Delivery Process			5.2 Process Management: Product and Service Production and Delivery			

Lean Management System	Lean Production Implementation Systems		Criteria of Major Quality and Productivity Awards			
Keys and Control Points	Hirano: JIT Implementation	Kobayashi: 20 Keys	Baldrige Award (ASQC)	Shingo Prize (NAM)	Deming Prize (JUSE)	PM Prize (JIPM)
2. Business Renewal		Key 2. Rationalizing the System/Management of Objectives	1.1 Senior Executive Leadership; 1.2 Leadership System and Organization	I.(A) Leading; II.(A) Manufacturing Vision and Strategy; II.(D) Manufacturing and Business Integration	1. Policies; 10. Future Plans	1. Policy and Target of TPM—Organization and Operation of TPM
2.1 Business Renewal	1. Awareness Revolution		2.2 Competitive Comparisons and Benchmarking; 3.1 Strategy Development; 7.1 Customer and Market Knowledge			
2.2 Focus			3.1 Strategy Development		1(2) Methods for establishing policies; 1(3) Appropriateness and consistency of policies; 7. Control/management	2 (1), 2(2) [equipment loss policy and current loss status]
2.3 Standardization			3.2 Strategy Deployment		1(5) Communication and dissemination of policies	
2.4 Adherence					2(7) Quality control/management diagnosis	
2.5 Reflection					1(6) Checks on policies and status of their achievement	

Lean Management System — Lean Production Implementation Systems — Criteria of Major Quality and Productivity Awards

Keys and Control Points	Hirano: JIT Implementation	Kobayashi: 20 Keys	Baldrige Award (ASQC)	Shingo Prize (NAM)	Deming Prize (JUSE)	PM Prize (JIPM)
3. Lean Organization		Key 2. Rationalizing the System/Management of Objectives	1.2 Leadership System and Organization; 4.2 High Performance Work Systems		2. The organization and its operations	1. Policy and Target of TPM—Organization and Operation of TPM
3.1 Team Activities		Key 3. Improvement Team Activities		I.(B) Empowering		1(9) [small group activities]; 2(5) [equipment improvement project teams]
3.2 Networked Organization					2(3) Interdepartmental coordination	
3.3 Rewards and Recognition						
3.4 Evaluation and Compensation						
3.5 Lean Administration			5.3 Process Management: Support Services			8. Office TPM

Lean Management System	Lean Production Implementation Systems		Criteria of Major Quality and Productivity Awards				
Keys and Control Points	Hirano: JIT Implementation	Kobayashi: 20 Keys	Baldrige Award (ASQC)	Shingo Prize (NAM)	Deming Prize (JUSE)	PM Prize (JIPM)
4. Partnering				I.(C) Partnering		
4.1 Employee Value		Key 14. Empowering Workers to Make Improvements	4.3 Human Resource Planning and Evaluation; 4.4 Employee Well-Being and Satisfaction	I.(B) Empowering		
4.2 Comakership		Key 12. Developing Your Suppliers	5.4 Management of Supplier Performance			
4.3 Environmental Impact		Key 19. Conserving Energy and Materials	1.3 Public Responsibility and Corporate Citizenship			9(9) Good pollution management systems...; 9(10) Emergency manual.... Emergency equipments....
4.4 Social Integrity			1.3 Public Responsibility and Corporate Citizenship			

Lean Management System	Lean Production Implementation Systems		Criteria of Major Quality and Productivity Awards			
Keys and Control Points	Hirano: JIT Implementation	Kobayashi: 20 Keys	Baldrige Award (ASQC)	Shingo Prize (NAM)	Deming Prize (JUSE)	PM Prize (JIPM)
5. Information Architecture		Key 18. Using Information Systems	2.1 Management of Information and Data	I.(A) Leading	4. Information gathering, communication and its utilization	
5.1 Workplace Organization and Visual Control	2. The 5 S's; 7. Visual Control	Key 1. Cleaning and Organization		II.(B) Manufacturing Process Integration		3. Jishu-Hozen [sometimes referred to as equipment 5S]
5.2 Fast Feedback Systems	10. Quality Assurance	Key 11. Quality Assurance System		II.(C) Quality and Productivity Methods Integration		
5.3 Performance Measurement		Key 2. Rationalizing the System/Management of Objectives	6.0 Business Results	III. Measured Quality and Productivity; IV. Measured Customer Satisfaction	9. Effects	10. Effects and Assessment of TPM
5.4 Kaizen Reporting				I.(B) Empowering	3(7) The system of improvement suggestions and its status	

Lean Management System	Lean Production Implementation Systems		Criteria of Major Quality and Productivity Awards			
Keys and Control Points	Hirano: JIT Implementation	Kobayashi: 20 Keys	Baldrige Award (ASQC)	Shingo Prize (NAM)	Deming Prize (JUSE)	PM Prize (JIPM)
6. Culture of Improvement		Key 6. Manufacturing Value Analysis	4.2 High Performance Work Systems	I.(B) Empowering		
6.1 Standardization	11. Standard Operations	Key 17. Efficiency Control			6. Standardization	
6.2 Waste-Free Strategy		Key 13. Elimination Waste (Treasure Map)		II.(B) Manufacturing Process Integration		
6.3 Technology Diffusion		Key 20. Leading Technology and Site Technology			3. Education and dissemination; 5. Analysis	7(7) [skill transfer]
6.4 Education			4.3 Employee Education, Training, and Development		3. Education and dissemination	7. Education and Training

Lean Management System | Lean Production Implementation Systems | Criteria of Major Quality and Productivity Awards

Keys and Control Points	Hirano: JIT Implementation	Kobayashi: 20 Keys	Baldrige Award (ASQC)	Shingo Prize (NAM)	Deming Prize (JUSE)	PM Prize (JIPM)
7. Lean Production			5.2 Process Management: Product and Service Production and Delivery	II.(B) Manufacturing Process Integration		
7.1 Flow Production	3. Flow Production	Key 4. Reducing Inventory (Shortening Lead Time)				
7.2 Multiprocess Handling	4. Multi-process Operation	Key 15. Skill Versatility and Cross-Training				
7.3 Leveled, Mixed Model Production	8. Level Production					
7.4 Quick Changeover	9. Changeover	Key 5. Quick Changeover Technology				
7.5 Automation with a Human Touch	12. Human Automation	Key 7. Zero Monitor Manufacturing				
7.6 Pull system/Coupled Production	6. Kanban	Key 8. Coupled Production				
7.7 Production Scheduling		Key 16. Production Scheduling				

Lean Management System	Lean Production Implementation Systems		Criteria of Major Quality and Productivity Awards			
Keys and Control Points	Hirano: JIT Implementation	Kobayashi: 20 Keys	Baldrige Award (ASQC)	Shingo Prize (NAM)	Deming Prize (JUSE)	PM Prize (JIPM)
8. Lean Equipment Management	13. Maintenance and Safety	Key 9. Maintaining Equipment		II.(B) Manufacturing Process Integration		
8.1 Equipment/Process Improvement						2. Focused Improvement
8.2 Autonomous Maintenance					8(6) Instrumentation and inspection	3. Autonomous Maintenance
8.3 Planned Maintenance						4. Planned Maintenance
8.4 Quality Maintenance				II.(C) Quality and Productivity Methods Integration	8(4) Process design, process analysis and process control and improvement	5. Quality Maintenance
8.5 Early Equipment Management						6. Early Product and Equipment Management
8.6 Safety					8(2) Preventive activities for safety and product liability	9. Safety, Hygiene, and Environmental Controls
8.7 Equipment Investment and Maintenance Prevention Design						6(6); 6(7) [MP design and feedback systems] 6(8) [equipment economics and risk analysis] 6(9) [equipment budget]

Lean Management System	Lean Production Implementation Systems		Criteria of Major Quality and Productivity Awards				
Keys and Control Points	Hirano: JIT Implementation	Kobayashi: 20 Keys	Baldrige Award (ASQC)	Shingo Prize (NAM)	Deming Prize (JUSE)	PM Prize (JIPM)
9. Lean Engineering						
9.1 Design Process			4.2 High Performance Work Systems	I.(B) Empowering		
9.2 Design for Quality, Cost, and Delivery			5.1 Design and Introduction of Products and Services	II.(B) Manufacturing Process Integration	8(1) New product and service development methods	6(1), 6(2), 6(3), 6(4),[initial management of product and equipment]

For Further Reading

Akao, Yoji. *Hoshin Kanri: Policy Deployment for Successful TQM.* Portland, Ore.: Productivity Press, 1991.

Deming Prize Committee, Union of Japanese Scientists and Engineers. "Deming Application Prize." *The Deming Prize Guide for Overseas Companies.* Tokyo: JUSE, 1992.

Funk, Jeffrey L. *The Teamwork Advantage: An Inside Look at Japanese Product and Technology Development.* Portland, Ore.: Productivity Press, 1992.

Galgano, Alberto. *Companywide Quality Management.* Portland, Ore.: Productivity Press, 1993.

Hirano, Hiroyuki. *JIT Implementation Manual.* Portland, Ore.: Productivity Press, 1991.

Japan Institute of Plant Maintenance. *PM Excellent Plant Awards, Check List B.* Tokyo: JIPM.

Kobayashi, Iwao. *20 Keys to Workplace Improvement,* revised ed. Portland, Ore.: Productivity Press, 1995.

Mather, Hal. *Competitive Manufacturing.* New York: Prentice Hall, 1988.

Meyer, Christopher. *Fast Cycle Time.* New York: Free Press, 1993.

Nakamura, Shigehiro. Unpublished talk delivered to the Xerox Mexicana Industrial Study Mission to Japan and Southeast Asia, 1994.

Nakamura, Shigehiro. *The New Standardization: Keystone of Continuous Improvement in Manufacturing.* Portland, Ore.: Productivity Press, 1993.

Nakhai, Behnam, and Joao Neves. "The Deming, Baldrige, and European Quality Awards." *Quality Progress,* April 1994, pp. 33-38.

Neves, Joao S., and Behnam Nakhai. "The Evolution of the Baldrige Award." *Quality Progress,* June 1994, pp. 65-70.

Northey, Patrick, and Nigel Southway. *Cycle Time Management: The Fast Track to Time-Based Productivity Improvement.* Portland, Ore.: Productivity Press, 1993.

The Oliver Wight ABCD Checklist for Operational Excellence, 4th ed. Essex Junction, Vt.: Oliver Wight, 1992.

Shiba, Shoji, Alan Graham, and David Walden. *A New American TQM: Four Practical Revolutions in Management.* Portland, Ore.: Productivity Press, 1993.

Shingo Prize for Excellence in Manufacturing. *1995–96 Application Guidelines.* Logan, Utah: Utah State University College of Business.

U.S. Department of Commerce/American Society for Quality Control. *Malcolm Baldrige National Quality Award: 1995 Award Criteria.*

About the Authors

THOMAS L. JACKSON

DR. JACKSON FIRST BECAME INTERESTED in business and economics while working as a lawyer at the Department of Energy, where he managed requests for exceptions to price regulations on gasoline during the Oil Crises of 1978. After leaving government in 1980, he studied economics and international business at Indiana University School of Business, and graduated with an M.B.A. and a Ph.D. in business economics.

In 1989, Dr. Jackson was asked to become a consulting editor for Productivity Press. Through his association with Productivity, he first became aware of the Toyota production system and the revolution it is causing throughout the business world. In 1991, Productivity CEO Norman Bodek invited him to become a manufacturing consultant overseas, and in 1992, Dr. Jackson became managing director of SEA Productivity Sdn. Bhd., a joint venture with Productivity, Inc. in southeast Asia. In 1995, he returned to the United States to become vice president of product development for Productivity, Inc. Dr. Jackson's clients include BHP Steel, Ford Motor Company, National Semiconductor, Nestle, Nissan, Otis Elevator, Pharmmalaysia, Perelli Cables (Australia), QDOS Microcircuits, and Xerox Mexicana. He lives with his wife, Daksha, in Portland, Oregon.

CONSTANCE E. DYER

A LAWYER BY TRAINING, CONNIE DYER is the director of TPM research and product development for Productivity, Inc. and Productivity Press. She is also director of research for the American Institute for Total Productive Maintenance (AITPM) and technical advisor for the *TPM Newsletter*. Certified in 1993 as a TPM Instructor by the Japan Institute of Plant Maintenance (JIPM), she has produced and delivered training in autonomous maintenance, equipment/process improvement, and TPM awareness education. Her training materials have been endorsed by top JIPM consultants and have launched and supported team improvement activities in many companies in the United States and abroad. Her writings have appeared in *Harvard Business Review, Quality Digest, P/PM Technology*, and the *TPM Newsletter*.

Ms. Dyer began her career in manufacturing improvement in 1984 as a trainer and designer for Productivity, Inc., specializing in shopfloor tools to support JIT implementation. In 1985, she produced the first training program on visual control systems outside of Japan. From 1986 to 1989, she was the editor of Productivity Press, and was responsible for the Shigeo Shingo series, the TPM series, and many other books on manufacturing improvement. She has traveled widely in Japan and has studied shopfloor improvement methods under the direction of leading Japanese consultants at both American and Japanese companies. She lives in Portland, Oregon.

Index

20 Keys to Workplace Improvement,
7, 31, 95

Action team, 5
Adherence, 3
Attitude, Delta Zero as an, 24–25
Audit
   Corporate Diagnosis, stages of,
     28–40
   president's, 5
   product quality, 2
Awards, 7, 31, 95–98

Best practices, 44–45
Bodek, Norman, ix
Business renewal, 2
   award criteria for, 100
   process of, 18–20, *19*

Capabilities, 2
CEO's diagnosis, 5
Concordances, *95–107*
Copernicus, 23

Cornerstones of growth, 10–11
Corporate Diagnosis, 1
   action team reports in, 4–5
   CEO's role in, 5–6
   and corporate growth, 2
   deployment team reports in, 5
   focal point of, 3–4
   graphic displays in, 7–8
   goals of, 4
   lean management and, 5
   scheduling the, 33
Corporate Diagnosis audit, 28–40
   analysis stage, 39
   preparation stage, 28
   recognition stage, 39
   site visit stage, 34, 37
Culture of improvement, 11, 15
   award criteria for, 104
   lean management reference
     tables for, *75–78*
   and work unit diagnosis, 33
Customer focus, 11, 13–14
   award criteria for, 99

lean management reference
  tables for, *54–56*

Delta Zero, 10
  as an attitude, 24–25
  learning and, 23–25
  as a principle, 24
Deming Application Prize, 2, 95,
  97
  address for, 98
Deployment, extent of, 45
Deployment team, 5
Development, nine keys to, 10
  and cornerstones of growth, 12
  profitability and, *13*
Development plan, *50*
Diagnostic form, 7
  for site visit, 34, *35*
  for autonomous maintenance
    control point, *36, 38*
  recording observations on, 37,
    38
Diagnostic Questions, 6, 29–33,
  30, 36, 53–94
Diagnostic scoring
  criteria for, 42, 44–46
  using progress tables for,
    41–42, 43
Diagnostic Scoring Matrix, 8, 46,
  47
Diagnostic team, 27–28
Disconnect, 46, 46*n*
Distribution, 19
Dyer, Constance, 112

Focus, 2–3

Goals, business, 1

Hewlett-Packard, 18–19
Hirano, Hiroyuki, 7, 31

*Implementing a Lean Management
  System*, 2, 20, 21, 37, 48

Information architecture, 11, 14
  award criteria for, 103
  lean management reference
    tables for, *70–74*
  and work unit diagnosis, 31
Integrated implementation, 1
Integration, cross-functional,
  45–46
ISO 9000, 2

Jackson, Thomas L., 111
JIT Implementation Manual, 7, 31,
  95
Just-in-time inventory, 1
  in business renewal process, 18
  and Delta Zero, 23
  and diagnostic scoring, 44

Kobayashi, Iwao, 7, 31

Leadership, 11, 14
  lean management reference
    tables for, *57–61*
Lean engineering, 11, 15
  award criteria for, 107
  lean management reference
    tables for, *93–94*
Lean equipment management,
  11, 15, 48
  award criteria for, 106
  concordance for, *32*
  lean management reference
    tables for, *86–92*
  and work unit diagnosis, 31
Lean management reference
  tables, *53–94*
Lean Management Scoreboard, 7,
  15, 48, *49*, 50
  control points on, 15
Lean Management System, 1
  action team reports in, 4–5
  Corporate Diagnosis in, 2–5
  deployment team reports in, 5
  elements of, 9

framework for, 10–17
and keys to development, 12
Progress Tables in, 6–7, 37,
    53–94
targets in, 27
Lean organization, 11, 14
award criteria for, 101
lean management reference
    tables for, *62–66*
and work unit diagnosis, 31
Lean production, 1, 11, 15
award criteria for, 105
lean management reference
    tables for, *79–85*
and Lean Management System,
    2
and work unit diagnosis, 31
Lean Radar Chart, 7, 51, *52*
Learning
Delta Zero and, 23–25
normal, 23
organizational, 15, 17–18
paradigmatic, 23
paradox of, 23
Lexus, 18

Malcolm Baldrige National
    Quality Award, 7, 95, 96
address for, 98
Market realities, 2
Market, 19
Mass production organizations,
    12
learning in, 15
Misconnect, 46, 46*n*
Mistake-proofing, 1
and diagnostic scoring, 44

Organizational learning, 15,
    17–18
Organizational structure, 2

Paradigm, 23
Partnering, 11, 14
award criteria for, 102

lean management reference
    tables for, *67–69*
and work unit diagnosis, 31
Plan-do-check-at cycle, 4
PM Excellence Prize, 95, 97
address for, 98
President's audit, 5
Process benchmarking, 44
Product price, 19
Product quality, 19
Product quality audit, 2
Product variety, 19
Progress Tables, 6–7, 8, 29, *30,* 31,
    37, *53–94*
in diagnostic scoring, 41–42, *43*

Questions, development of, 28,
    29, 31, 33
Quick changeover, 2
and diagnostic scoring, 44

Radar Charts, 7, 51, *52*
Reengineering, 18, 19
Reflection, 3
Reliable method, 44–45
Report, from diagnosed unit, 29,
    33–34
Reports
action team, 4–5
deployment team, 5
Results criterion, 46

Scores, determining, 6
Scoring criteria
extent of cross-functional inte-
    gration, 42, 45–46
extent of deployment, 42, 45
reliable method, 42, 44–45
results, 42, 46
Shin-Etsu Chemical Industry, 2
Shingo Prize for Excellence in
    Manufacturing, 95, 96
address for, 98
Standardization, 3, 5

Strategic Improvement Cycle,
    2–3, 10, *22*
    graphic displays for, 7
    phases of, 20–21
Strategic management system, 2
Strategic planning, 2
    and Business Renewal Process,
        19
Strategy, 2
    as cornerstone of growth, 10, 11
    and Corporate Diagnosis, 27
    and work unit diagnosis, 33
Strengths, 2
    as cornerstone of growth, 10, 11
    keys to, 14–15
Structure, 2
    as cornerstone of growth, 10, 11
System development, 17
System excellence, 17

System initiation, 15, 17
System maturity, 17
System, 9

Top management team, 5
    in Corporate Diagnosis, 27
Total productive maintenance
    (TPM), 1
    and Delta Zero, 22
    and diagnostic scoring, 44
Total quality management, 1
    and diagnostic scoring, 44
Toyota Motor Company, 2, 18, 23

Vision, 2
    in Corporate Diagnosis, 27

Waste, 10, 18
Work unit diagnosis, 31, 33, *40*

BOOKS FROM PRODUCTIVITY PRESS

Productivity Press publishes books that empower individuals and companies to achieve excellence in quality, productivity, and the creative involvement of all employees. Through steadfast efforts to support the vision and strategy of continuous improvement, Productivity Press delivers today's leading-edge tools and techniques gathered directly from industrial leaders around the world.

Call toll-free 1-800-394-6868 for our free catalog.

IMPLEMENTING A LEAN MANAGEMENT SYSTEM

Thomas L. Jackson with Constance E. Dyer

Does your company think and act ahead of technological change, ahead of the customer, and ahead of the competition? Thinking strategically requires a company to face these questions with a clear future image of itself. *Implementing a Lean Management System* lays out a comprehensive management system for aligning the firm's vision of the future with market realities. Based on hoshin management, the Japanese strategic planning method used by top managers for driving TQM throughout an organization, *Lean Management* is about deploying vision, strategy, and policy to all levels of daily activity. It is an eminently practical methodology emerging out of the implementation of continuous improvement methods and employee involvement. The key tools of this book builds on the knowledge of the worker, multiskilling, and an understanding of the role and responsibilities of the new lean manufacturer.
ISBN 1-56327-085-4 / 182 pages / $65.00 / Order ILMS-B257

HOSHIN KANRI
Policy Deployment for Successful TQM

Yoji Akao (ed.)

Hoshin kanri, the Japanese term for policy deployment, is an approach to strategic planning and quality improvement that has become a pillar of Total Quality Management (TQM) for a growing number of U.S. firms. This book compiles examples of policy deployment that demonstrates how company vision is converted into individual responsibility. It includes practical guidelines, 150 charts and diagrams, and five case studies that illustrate the procedures of *hoshin kanri*. The six steps to advanced process planning are reviewed and include a five-year vision, one-year plan, deployment to departments, execution, monthly audit, and annual audit.
ISBN 0-915299-57-7 / 241 pages / $65.00 / Order HOSHIN-B257

Productivity Press, Dept. BK, P.O. Box 13390, Portland, OR 97213-0390
Telephone: 1-800-394-6868   Fax: 1-800-394-6286

IMPLEMENTING TPM

The North American Experience

Charles J. Robinson and Andrew P. Ginder

The authors document an approach to TPM planning and deployment that modifies the JIPM 12-step process to accommodate the experiences of North American plants. They include details and advice on specific deployment steps, OEE calculation methodology, and autonomous maintenance deployment. This book shows how to make TPM work in unionized plants and how to position TPM to support and complement other strategic manufacturing improvement initiatives.
ISBN 1-56327-087-0 / 224 pages / $45.00 / Order IMPTPM-257

THE IMPROVEMENT ENGINE

Creativity and Innovation Through Employee Involvement—The Kaizen Teian System

JHRA (ed.)

The Improvement Engine offers the most all inclusive information available today on this proven method for increasing employee involvement. Kaizen Teian is a technique developed in Japan for encouraging employees to constantly look for and make improvement suggestions. This book explores the subtleties between designing a moderately successful program and a highly successful one and includes a host of tools, techniques, and case studies.
ISBN 1-56327-010-2 / 155 pages / $40.00 / Order IMPENG-B257

REVISED!
20 KEYS TO WORKPLACE IMPROVEMENT

Iwao Kobayashi

The 20 Keys system does more than just bring together twenty of the world's top manufacturing improvement approaches—it integrates these individual methods into a closely interrelated system for revolutionizing every aspect of your manufacturing organization. This revised edition of Kobayashi's bestseller amplifies the synergistic power of raising the levels of all these critical areas simultaneously. The new edition presents upgraded criteria for the five-level scoring system in most of the 20 Keys, supporting your progress toward becoming not only best in your industry but best in the world. New material and an updated layout throughout assist managers in implementing this comprehensive approach. In addition, valuable case studies describe how Morioka Seiko (Japan) advanced in Key 18 (use of microprocessors) and how Windfall Products (Pennsylvania) adapted the 20 Keys to its situation with good results.
ISBN 1-56327-109-5/302 pages / $50.00 / Order 20KREV-B257

Productivity Press, Dept. BK, P.O. Box 13390, Portland, OR 97213-0390
Telephone: 1-800-394-6868   Fax: 1-800-394-6286

COST REDUCTION SYSTEMS
Target Costing and Kaizen Costing
Yasuhiro Monden

Yasuhiro Monden provides a solid framework for implementing two powerful cost reduction systems that have revolutionized Japanese manufacturing management: target costing and kaizen costing. Target costing is a cross-functional system used during the development and design stage for new products. Kaizen costing focuses on cost reduction activities for existing products throughout their life cycles, drawing on approaches such as value analysis. Used together, target costing and kaizen costing form a complete cost reduction system that can be applied from the product's conception to the end of its life cycle. These methods are applicable to both discrete manufacturing and process industries.
ISBN 1-56327-068-4 / 400 pages / $50.00 / Order CRS-B257

CEDAC
A Tool for Continuous Systematic Improvement
Ryuji Fukuda

CEDAC® encompasses three tools for continuous systematic improvement: window analysis (for identifying problems), the CEDAC diagram (a modification of the classic "fishbone diagram," for analyzing problems and developing standards), and window development (for ensuring adherence to standards). This manual provides directions for setting up and using CEDAC. Sample forms included.
ISBN 0-915299-26-7 / 144 pages / $55.00 / Order CEDAC-B257

CONCURRENT ENGINEERING
Shortening Lead Times, Raising Quality, and Lowering Costs
John R. Hartley

By simultaneously taking into account the concerns of design, production, purchasing, finance, and marketing from the very first stages of product planning, concurrent engineering makes doing it right the first time the rule instead of the exception. An introductory handbook, this text gives managers 16 clear guidelines for achieving concurrent engineering and provides abundant case studies of Japanese, U.S., and European successes.
ISBN 1-56327-006-4 / 330 pages / $60.00 / Order CONC-B257

FAST FOCUS ON TQM
A Concise Guide to Companywide Learning
Derm Barrett

Finally, here's one source for all your TQM questions. Compiled in this concise, easy-to-read handbook are definitions and detailed explanations of over 160 key terms used in TQM. Organized in a simple alphabetical glossary form, the book can be used either as a primer for anyone being introduced to TQM or as a complete reference guide. It helps to align teams, departments, or entire organizations in a common understanding and use of TQM terminology. For anyone entering or currently involved in TQM, this is one resource you must have.
ISBN 1-56327-049-8 / 186 pages / $20.00 / Order FAST-B257

Productivity Press, Dept. BK, P.O. Box 13390, Portland, OR 97213-0390
Telephone: 1-800-394-6868   **Fax: 1-800-394-6286**

CYCLE TIME MANAGEMENT
The Fast Track to Time-Based Productivity Improvement
Patrick Northey and Nigel Southway

As much as 90 percent of the operational activities in a traditional plant are nonessential or pure waste. This book presents a proven methodology for eliminating this waste within 24 to 30 months by measuring productivity in terms of time instead of revenue or people. CTM is a cohesive management strategy that integrates just-in-time (JIT) production, computer integrated manufacturing (CIM), and total quality control (TQC). From this succinct, highly focused book, you'll learn what CTM is, how to implement it, and how to manage it.
ISBN 1-56327-015-3 / 200 pages / $35.00 / Order CYCLE-B257

DESIGN TEAM REVOLUTION
How to Cut Lead Times in Half and Double Your Productivity
Kenichi Sekine and Keisuke Arai

This book addresses the problem of waste in the product design process. It shows how to apply continuous improvement methods that have been successful on the shop floor to the design function, to eliminate waste in time, materials, transport, and other areas. The authors show design managers how to establish one-piece flow, U-cell processes, and parallel design for design teams, and discuss the role of running changes, site diagnosis and machine inspection, and designer training.
ISBN 1-56327-008-0 / 328 pages / $85.00 / Order DTREV-B257

HANDBOOK FOR PRODUCTIVITY MEASUREMENT AND IMPROVEMENT
William F. Christopher and Carl G. Thor, eds.

An unparalleled resource! In over 100 chapters, nearly 80 front-runners in the quality movement reveal the evolving theory and specific practices of world class organizations. Spanning a wide variety of industries and business sectors, they discuss quality and productivity in manufacturing, service industries, profit centers, administration, nonprofit and government institutions, health care and education. Contributors include Robert C. Camp, Peter F. Drucker, Jay W. Forrester, Joseph M. Juran, Robert S. Kaplan, John W. Kendrick, Yasuhiro Monden, and Lester C. Thurow. Comprehensive in scope and organized for easy reference, this compendium belongs in every company and academic institution concerned with business and industrial viability.
ISBN 1-56327-007-2 / 1344 pages / $90.00 / Order HPM-B257

JIT FACTORY REVOLUTION
A Pictorial Guide to Factory Design of the Future
Hiroyuki Hirano

The first encyclopedic picture-book of Just-In-Time, using photos and diagrams to show exactly how JIT looks and functions in production and assembly plants. Unprecedented behind-the-scenes look at multi-process handling, cell technology, quick changeovers, kanban, andon, and other visual control systems. See why a picture is worth a thousand words.
ISBN 0-915299-44-5 / 218 pages / $50.00 / Order JITFAC-B257

Productivity Press, Dept. BK, P.O. Box 13390, Portland, OR 97213-0390
Telephone: 1-800-394-6868　　　　　　　　　　**Fax: 1-800-394-6286**

LEARNING ORGANIZATIONS
Developing Cultures for Tomorrow's Workplace
Sarita Chawla and John Renesch, Editors

The ability to learn faster than your competition may be the only sustainable competitive advantage! A learning organization is one where people continually expand their capacity to create results they truly desire, where new and expansive patterns of thinking are nurtured, where collective aspiration is set free, and where people are continually learning how to learn together. This compilation of 34 powerful essays, written by recognized experts worldwide, is rich in concept and theory as well as application and example. An inspiring followup to Peter Senge's groundbreaking bestseller *The Fifth Discipline*, these essays are grouped in four sections that address all aspects of learning organizations: the guiding ideas behind systems thinking; the theories, methods, and processes for creating a learning organization; the infrastructure of the learning model; and arenas of practice.
ISBN 1-56327-110-9 / 575 pages / $35.00 / Order LEARN-B257

MANUFACTURING STRATEGY
John Miltenburg

This book offers a step-by-step method for creating a strategic manufacturing plan. The key tool is a multidimensional worksheet that links the competitive analysis to manufacturing outputs, the seven basic production systems, the levels of capability and the levers for moving to a higher level. The author presents each element of the worksheet and shows you how to link them to create an integrated strategy and implementation plan. By identifying the appropriate production system for your business, you can determine what output you can expect from manufacturing, how to improve outputs, and how to change to more optimal production systems as your business needs changes. This is a valuable book for general managers, operations managers, engineering managers, marketing managers, comptrollers, consultants, and corporate staff in any manufacturing company.
ISBN 1-56327-071-4 / 391 pages / $45.00 / Item # MANST-B257

A NEW AMERICAN TQM
Four Practical Revolutions in Management
Shoji Shiba, Alan Graham, and David Walden

For TQM to succeed in America, you need to create an American-style "learning organization" with the full commitment and understanding of senior managers and executives. Written expressly for this audience, *A New American TQM* offers a comprehensive and detailed explanation of TQM and how to implement it, based on courses taught at MIT's Sloan School of Management and the Center for Quality Management, a consortium of American companies. Full of case studies and amply illustrated, the book examines major quality tools and how they are being used by the most progressive American companies today.
ISBN 1-56327-032-3 / 606 pages / $50.00 / Order NATQM-B257

Productivity Press, Dept. BK, P.O. Box 13390, Portland, OR 97213-0390
Telephone: 1-800-394-6868   **Fax: 1-800-394-6286**

ONE-PIECE FLOW
Cell Design for Transforming the Production Process
Kenichi Sekine

By reconfiguring your traditional assembly lines into production cells based on one-piece flow, you can drastically reduce your lead time, manpower requirements, and number of defects. Sekine examines the basic principles of process flow building, then offers detailed case studies of how various industries designed unique one-piece flow systems to meet their particular needs.
ISBN 0-915299-33-X / 308 pages / $75.00 / Order 1PIECE-B257

PERFORMANCE MEASUREMENT FOR WORLD CLASS MANUFACTURING
A Model for American Companies
Brian H. Maskell

If your company is adopting world class manufacturing techniques, you'll need new methods of performance measurement to control production variables. In practical terms, this book describes the new methods of performance measurement and how they are used in a changing environment. For manufacturing managers as well as cost accountants, it provides a theoretical foundation of these innovative methods supported by extensive practical examples. The book specifically addresses performance measures for delivery, process time, production flexibility, quality, and finance.
ISBN 0-915299-99-2 / 448 pages / $55.00 / Order PERFM-B257

A REVOLUTION IN MANUFACTURING
The SMED System
Shigeo Shingo

The heart of JIT is quick changeover methods. Dr. Shingo, inventor of the Single-Minute Exchange of Die (SMED) system for Toyota, shows you how to reduce your changeovers by an average of 98 percent! By applying Shingo's techniques, you'll see rapid improvements (lead time reduced from weeks to days, lower inventory and warehousing costs) that will improve quality, productivity, and profits.
ISBN 0-915299-03-8 / 383 pages / $80.00 / Order SMED-B257

Productivity Press, Dept. BK, P.O. Box 13390, Portland, OR 97213-0390
Telephone: 1-800-394-6868   **Fax: 1-800-394-6286**

TO ORDER: Write, phone, or fax Productivity Press, Dept. BK, P.O. Box 13390, Portland, OR 97213-0390, phone 1-800-394-6868, fax 1-800-394-6286. Send check or charge to your credit card (American Express, Visa, MasterCard accepted).

U.S. ORDERS: Add $5 shipping for first book, $2 each additional for UPS surface delivery. Add $5 for each AV program containing 1 or 2 tapes; add $12 for each AV program containing 3 or more tapes. We offer attractive quantity discounts for bulk purchases of individual titles; call for more information.

ORDER BY E-MAIL: Order 24 hours a day from anywhere in the world. Use either address:

> To order: **service@ppress.com**

> To view the online catalog and/or order: **http://www.ppress.com/**

INTERNATIONAL ORDERS: Write, phone, or fax for quote and indicate shipping method desired. For international callers, telephone number is 503-235-0600 and fax number is 503-235-0909. Prepayment in U.S. dollars must accompany your order (checks must be drawn on U.S. banks). When quote is returned with payment, your order will be shipped promptly by the method requested.

NOTE: Prices are in U.S. dollars and are subject to change without notice.

Product-Market Matrix

Workcenter Control Board

vision

CORPORATE DIAGNOSIS

Delta Zero

system development

structure

Analysis Summary

control points

lean engineering

Lean Management Se

ployment Plan

action team

lean production

Team Action Plan

customer focus

mass producti

strategy

Daily Planner

system development

Key Factor Matrix

lean organization

Monthly Self-Reports

three cornerstones of growth

strengths

Development Plan

Monthly Planner

LEAN RADAR CHART

WORKCENTER CONTROL

Strategic

Business Renewal Process

deployment team

FOCUS

contro

checkpoints

five levels of